CREATIVE
PROJECT
MANAGEMENT

Innovative Project Options to Solve Problems On Time and Under Budget

MICHAEL S. DOBSON
AUTHOR OF *STREETWISE PROJECT MANAGEMENT*

AND
TED LEEMANN

New York   Chicago   San Francisco   Lisbon   London
Madrid   Mexico City   Milan   New Delhi   San Juan
Seoul   Singapore   Sydney   Toronto

The McGraw·Hill Companies

Copyright © 2010 by The McGraw-Hill Companies. All rights reserved. Printed in the
United States of America. Except as permitted under the United States Copyright Act of
1976, no part of this publication may be reproduced or distributed in any form or by any
means, or stored in a data base or retrieval system, without the prior written permission
of the publisher.

1 2 3 4 5 6 7 8 9 0   DOC/DOC   1 5 4 3 2 1 0

ISBN   978-0-07-173933-7
MHID 0-07-173933-5

Illustrations by Baker & Hill Graphic Design.
Photo credits: p. 35, AP Images/Harry Hall; p. 122, AP Images; all other photographs,
Wikimedia Commons.

McGraw-Hill books are available at special quantity discounts to use as premiums and sales
promotions, or for use in corporate training programs. To contact a representative, please
e-mail us at bulksales@mcgraw-hill.com.

This book is printed on acid-free paper.

This book is dedicated to my dear friend
Humayun Mirza.

Michael Dobson

To my wife, Sandy, and family, and to my parents,
Doris and Edwin.

Ted Leemann

Contents

Acknowledgments

It takes a village to produce a book. Thanks (and a tip o' the hat) to the many people who contributed ideas, tools, insights, and operational help, including Mark Hill of Baker and Hill Graphic Design, who turned our rough concepts into works of art; Maryann Karinch, who came to the rescue of Chapter 7 with management insights about the business of intelligence from her new book with Peter Earnest, executive director of the International Spy Museum and former senior CIA national clandestine service officer; Misha Burnett, the Eric Hoffer of locksmithing, who invented the model showing consequences of mismatching authority and responsibility in Chapter 8; and Robert Coulter for offering perspective and insight from a different generation.

The team at McGraw-Hill has been a professional delight to work with. John Aherne, our acquisitions editor, and Joe Berkowitz, our project editor, provided sure guidance and insightful questions. Janice Race's ace copyediting team caught just about everything else. Our literary agent Maryann Karinch of The Rudy Agency (an author in her own right, as noted above), coordinated all the myriad details of the project admirably.

And, of course, we'd like to thank the Academy. "King of the world, Ma!"

There are many others we need to thank, but they're playing the exit music, so it's time to go.

All mistakes and misjudgments that may have survived the eagle eye of our editors are, of course, our responsibility.

Except typos. Those pesky things breed on printing presses.

Why Do 70 Percent of Projects Fail?

We should be careful to get out of an experience only the wisdom that is
in it—and stop there; lest we be the cat that sits down on a hot stove-lid.
She will never sit down on a hot stove-lid again—and that is well;
but she will also never sit down on a cold one anymore.
—Mark Twain, *Following the Equator*, 1897

Why Projects Fail

If project management is such a good idea, why do 70 percent of all projects
fail, including those led by experienced and capable project managers?
Why does it seem to be so difficult to get projects done within the Triple
Constraints of time, cost, and performance—or, in layperson's language,
on time, on budget, and to spec?

Here are a few instructive examples of some of the more recent spec-
tacular failures in project management:

- In 2006, a $400 million purchasing system for Ford Motor Com-
pany was simply abandoned.

- Software errors in a U.K. Inland Revenue system resulted in a
$3.45 billion tax-credit overpayment.

- The infamous automated baggage system at Denver International

Airport burned through $250 million before being abandoned as unworkable.

■ The U.S. Department of Defense's $6 billion Kinetic Energy Interceptor program was terminated in 2009 after it was determined that it would not achieve its goals.

That's not all. Let's look at some numbers on project performance, compiled by the Standish Group. This organization has tracked project performance since 1994. Every two years, the Standish Group issues the CHAOS Report, which analyzes projects primarily in the software area. In the 2009 CHAOS Report, they reported these abysmal numbers:

■ 32 percent of projects were delivered on time, on budget, and with the required features and functions.

■ 44 percent were finished either late, over budget, or only partially completed.

■ 24 percent failed altogether, and they were canceled or abandoned.

There's good news and bad news here. The good news is that in 1994, when the Standish Group began tracking data, only 16 percent of projects succeeded in meeting the Triple Constraints (on time, on budget, to spec). On the other hand, the 2009 report shows that there's been a downtick in success (34 percent to 32 percent) and a significant uptick in failure (from a low of 15 percent to 24 percent).

For challenged projects, those that succeed in some elements and fail in others, the good news is that average budget overrun has dropped from 180 percent to only 43 percent. On the less positive side, time overruns have gone up 30 percent, and the percentage of features that have made it into the final product has dropped from 67 percent to 52 percent.

During this time, nearly 260,000 project managers earned the prestigious Project Management Professional (PMP) designation from the Project Management Institute (PMI). But the track record of improved project performance is lackluster at best.

What's going on?

A significant amount of study and reporting going back several decades has shed light on some of the reasons for these failures:

- The 1998 Bull survey, conducted by the French computer company Bull, identified the major causes of information technology (IT) project failure as a breakdown of communications, a lack of planning, and poor quality control.

- KPMG Canada, in 1997, identified the core project failure issues as poor planning, weak business case, and a lack of top management involvement and support.

- The Standish Group's 1995 CHAOS Report named incomplete requirements and lack of user involvement as reasons for project failure.

- The OASIG Study, published in 1995 by a U.K. group studying organizational aspects of information technology, cited lack of attention to the human and organizational aspects, poor project management, and poor articulation of user requirements as reasons why projects failed.

But poor planning, weak business case, and inattention to human and organizational aspects aren't *causes*; rather, they are *symptoms* of a much large systemic shortcoming. Treating the symptoms isn't the same as treating the underlying conditions. We know some of the root causes. People with poor interpersonal or team leadership skills create friction, as well as stakeholder conflict, in the project environment. Friction then increases inefficiency and waste. The size and complexity of an organization increases its moment of inertia, and getting anything to move takes enormous effort. People come and go, missions mutate, information goes missing, and ultimately entropy increases—we tend to move from order toward chaos.

Things fall apart. It's been said that there are only two reasons for project failure:

1. Things that nobody thought of or prepared for
2. Things that everybody thought of, but nobody did anything about

If you think about it, these reasons alone cover almost every potential incident. How often have you experienced project problems because a couple of the people working on your project were suddenly pulled off halfway through? How about a major change ordered in one or more of the Triple Constraints when the project is three-quarters completed? Perhaps there's some recurrent problem in the project environment that manages to happen every single time. Things take longer than you expected. Not everybody is really on board. There's always a layer of technical complexity no one expected. Stakeholders don't really know what they want, or they expect you to figure it out magically. All of these problems have the same result: a mess.

But do you account for these situations in your project planning? For a few outstanding project managers, the answer is at least a partial yes. For most of us, the answer rests somewhere between seldom and never.

Four Essential Project Questions

If you take the list of reasons from the studies mentioned previously, you can boil them down into the following four (often unasked) questions:

1. Why are we doing this? (Business case)
2. Who has an interest in what we're doing, and what do they each want and need? (Human and organizational aspects)
3. What do we have to do, and how are we going to do it? (Project management, including planning and quality control)
4. Who needs to be involved, and in what way? (Top management and user involvement and support)

The official standards of professional project management are designed to make sure these issues get appropriate consideration. But these considerations are quite obvious—it shouldn't take a PMP to grasp these concepts. Why, then, given the amount of effort, knowledge, and resources, is the situation in some ways getting *worse?*

The Operational Art of Project Management

The Project Management Institute (PMI) defines project management as "the application of knowledge, skills, tools, and techniques to project activities to meet project requirements." That's fine, but it's not nearly enough. Tools matter, of course, but a hammer and saw don't make someone a carpenter. Nor does mastery of technical skills alone ensure success.

To us, the key issue is *thinking well*—a focus on practical creativity that combines brainstorming, operational analysis, and planning to help you solve problems, find opportunities, and gain insights into any project.

Thinking well is a broad topic that includes many issues of interest to project managers, for example:

■ Thinking outside the box (or for Triple Constraints–oriented project managers, thinking outside the triangle)

■ Thinking clearly about the circumstances and environment in which our project takes place

■ Thinking honestly about risks and opportunities

■ Thinking about our own biases and blind spots so we can minimize their harmful effects

What project managers learn (some of us do so the hard way) is that the self-imposed constraints, assumptions, and opinions we and other stakeholders bring to the project manifest themselves subliminally in a variety of ways that too often hinder project performance.

Fundamentally, project management is an *operational art*; it's the link between strategy and tactics. Project management is the operational art that applies the goals of the project to the tasks we perform. Just as there's an operational art to getting an army (equivalent to a small city) to move, there's an operational art to building a skyscraper or leading a large IT project.

The Seven Dimensions of Project Management

Projects differ from operational work because projects *end*. By definition, they are "temporary and unique." Projects take place under constraints. Projects have different levels of complexity and different levels of uncertainty. Project managers live in a bounded, finite universe ruled by scarcity and governed by the Triple Constraints of time, cost, and performance, as shown in Figure 1-1.

The Triple Constraints themselves array in a hierarchy of driver, middle, and weak constraints. The driver is the leg of the Triple Constraints that drives the project. If you're rushing to beat the clock, time is the driver. If there's only so much money and not a penny more, cost is the driver. If getting it exactly right is essential, performance is the driver. The weak constraint, on the other hand, is not necessarily the least important constraint, but it is always the most flexible. That flexibility is where many creative solutions tend to live, so knowing not only which constraint is weak but where it is weak is a huge opportunity for any project manager. The middle is, well, in the middle. There may be exploitable flexibility, but not as much.

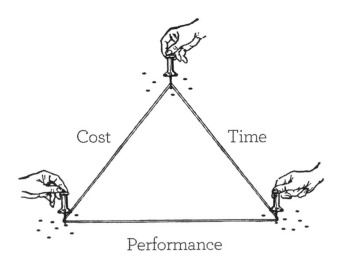

Figure 1-1. The Triple Constraints are the outer borders of any project: "How long do I have?" "How much can I spend?" and "What exactly does this puppy have to do, anyway?"

Each of the six possible combinations of time, cost, and performance forms a separate dimension of project management (Dobson/Feickert, 2007) and provides its own set of challenges and opportunities.

A Man, A Plan, A Gantt—Project Management

When the only tool you have is a hammer, all problems start to look like nails. The tendency to overuse the familiar tool (as opposed to the correct one) is part of our general proneness to prefer the familiar to the strange, the known to the unknown.

That line of thinking is a mistake. A creative project manager must accept that not everything is, can be, or should be familiar, known, or controllable. To understand how formal project management can mislead its modern practitioners, a brief history of its origins is necessary. Project management grew out of a production and engineering environment. In the process, rules, more rules, and even more rules were created. Project management is not production, however; it is the application of a standard production process to a unique and creative event. We tend to manage the creativity out of projects that are by definition unique and creative. That is the root cause of many project problems.

The project management profession has focused, reasonably enough, on performance improvement. To that end, the act of project management has been deconstructed, sliced and diced, and studied from a multitude of vantage points and technical specialties. The result has been a consistent effort to demystify project management by documenting centralized processes, to apply the rubric of "scientific management" so that projects become repeatable and controllable. It's a worthy goal. We question whether it is a realistic one.

Today, the center of gravity of the project management world is the Project Management Institute. In 2008, it reported a membership of 260,000 practitioners operating in 171 countries. PMI's standard reference, *A Guide to the Project Management Body of Knowledge* (popularly known as the *PMBOK Guide*) is the bible for people hoping to earn the designation of Project Management Professional by passing a challenging examination. This guide is an intellectual heir to the theory of scientific management.

In the 1880s and 1890s, Frederick W. Taylor pioneered the systematic analysis of workflows, hypothesizing that traditions and rules of thumb were insufficient to manage the radical new technologies brought on by the industrial age. That examination was scientific in that its conclusions were developed through careful study and analysis, not based on the whim or preference of any specific worker. This process of scientific management, Taylor believed, would naturally result in increased efficiency and productivity, combined with lower waste.

Taylorism and modern project management were joined at birth. Projects, of course, are as old as human civilization, but the story of project management as a formal discipline begins with Henry Lawrence Gantt (1861–1919), an American mechanical engineer and management consultant. Gantt, famous for the eponymous Gantt chart, was Frederick W. Taylor's college roommate and later worked with Taylor to apply scientific management to the steel industry.

Besides his chart, Henry Gantt is famous for two other accomplishments. He is credited as the originator of the idea of linking management bonuses to how well the managers have taught their employees to improve performance, and he established a formal model for industrial efficiency.

You Say You Want an Industrial Revolution . . .

Both Taylor and Gantt were children of the Industrial Revolution, a transformational moment in human history. Old ideas about work crumbled under the impact of new technology, and processes had to change. Unlike agriculture, in which a farmer can do everything right and still have a crop fall victim to a natural disaster like an early winter or a prolonged drought, the Industrial Revolution held out the hope of certainty. Machines, at least in theory, are predictable, repeatable, and efficient. If only workers could learn to be more like machines, we would shortly all live in a brave new world of controlled and managed happiness.

It's absolutely true that scientific management tamed the new technology of the Industrial Revolution, created new and valuable ideas about productivity and efficiency, and made the world a better place. It's equally true that there are downsides and costs associated with the new goals of the modern age. From Aldous Huxley's *Brave New World* to George Orwell's *1984*, from Fritz Lang's *Metropolis* to Charlie Chaplin's *Modern Times*, scientific management and the Industrial Revolution have been portrayed as dehumanizing workers and imposing tyrannical control over the smallest details of human behavior.

There's plenty of truth to go around.

In the field of risk management, we talk about "secondary risk," the new risk inadvertently created by your attempt to mitigate the original risk. It's well known that solutions often create new problems.

Mechanical metaphors can only take us so far. Even an infinite set of checklists, databases, and Intranet sites filled with updated Microsoft Project or Primavera files and a fully staffed Project Management Office (PMO) filled with certified PMPs have clearly not solved the problem of failed projects and in some ways make it worse.

At one time it was possible for an educated person to learn almost everything there was to learn. That hasn't been the case since the late Renaissance period, and as a result people have specialized. Specialization allows people to develop great expertise, but it complicates creative cross-border thinking and creates its own special cognitive bias, known as *déformation professionnelle*. That's when people look at every problem through their own narrow lens, forgetting that any other points of view exist.

Adaptability

The conflict between Theory X and Theory Y, between chains of command and the matrix organization, and between efficiency and teams has kept the authors and publishers of management books in business for generations, for which everyone associated with *Creative Project Management* is deeply grateful. Like all attempts to perform balancing acts on slippery slopes, we must make continual adjustments. Sometimes these adjustments are a function of attitude and temperament; sometimes they are a function of a shifting environment or the characteristics and constraints of the project.

It is well known that project management must be scaled, but it must also be stretched.

The systems and processes needed to manage the construction of a new aircraft carrier would be gross overkill if they were used to build a patio in one's backyard. Both projects are temporary and unique. Both can be broken down into packages of work. Both have measurable end states. But that's about all they have in common. Scale affects costs, and it limits your choices.

Projects in creative or design fields often require agile approaches. When the border between tasks blurs into a transition, when the work iterates instead of progresses, and when collaboration crosses boundaries at will, project management must also be stretched. The systems management virtues of formal methodology weaken, and uncertainty replaces it.

This outcome makes many traditional project managers extremely uncomfortable.

The Mental Effects of Uncertainty

The American National Standards Institute (ANSI) accredits PMI's *PMBOK Guide* as a standard for project management practice. That means its mission, in some ways, is to finish what Henry Gantt started: to ensure that the characteristics and performance of processes are consistent and that people use the same definitions and terms. It is fully compatible with Gantt's concept that industrial efficiency can only be produced by the application of scientific analysis to *all* aspects of the work in progress.

Like Henry Gantt, PMI appears to believe that the essential goal and aim of project management is to *eliminate chance and accidents*.

We believe that not only is that goal impossible but it is also not necessarily even a good idea.

The Chaos Paradigm

The age of machines has pointed the way toward a utopia of predictability, but in the age of computers and biotechnology, chaos seems much more the norm. While it's a good idea to tame what can usefully and practically be tamed, most of the project world lives where the wild things are. Chance and accidents have given us penicillin, vulcanized rubber, and that most essential tool for modern project managers, the Post-it Note. (You can have our copies of Microsoft Project, but you'll have to pry the Post-it Notes out of our cold, dead fingers.)

On top of that, the world in which we live sometimes resembles *Matrix Revolution* more than Industrial Revolution. The *fin de siècle* inevitably turns, sooner or later, into the Y2K problem. Gantt gives way to PERT (Project Evaluation and Review Technique), and PERT gives way to the Monte Carlo simulation technique. Statistical process control begets TQM (Total Quality Management), which begets ISO-9000, which begets lean Six Sigma (or as we like call it, "TQM with karate belts").

The center cannot hold.

We are living through a transformation easily equal to the Industrial Revolution, and uncertainty is our daily companion. But fear is not the only legitimate response to uncertainty, and it's frequently not the best one, either. Uncertainty also allows for hope.

We believe that embracing the reality of uncertainty and fluidity in the projects we manage, rather than fighting a forlorn attempt to stamp it out altogether, provides greater benefits, on the whole. Pretending to have a false certainty is no virtue. You have to sail the turbulent seas toward a destination that often shifts.

The Cost of Information

Project management, like most formal systems, has a side no one likes to talk about: it's expensive. Gathering, organizing, formatting, displaying, discussing, and using information takes time and money—often quite a lot of both. Formal project management can be dizzying in its breadth, in that it's supposed to cover everything. But don't think you have to drive carpet tacks with a sledgehammer. You can balance and adjust the tools you use based on the difficulty of your project.

In order to do that, you must ask this next question.

What Makes This Project Hard?

As Figure 1-2 shows, project challenge can be grouped into three rough dimensions:

1. **Constraints.** How tight are the constraints of time, cost, and performance?

2. **Complexity.** How complex is the project (tasks, resources, technology)?

3. **Certainty.** How much do we know about the risks and issues we face (on a continuum from certain to uncertain)?

Constraints

"Give me a lever long enough and a fulcrum on which to place it, and I shall move the world," said Archimedes. Of course, he couldn't have either one, and that's the reality of project management.

When we say "nothing's impossible," we generally mean something like this: given unlimited time, unlimited resources, and really flexible standards, we can accomplish anything. Well, okay. But that's seldom the reality of the situation. A job can be relatively easy if the constraints are loose, but it can be completely impossible if they are too tight. We rarely get to decide how those constraints are drawn. So, then, the first necessary step is to define the constraints: what *can't* you do, and how can you do it anyway?

Constraints can be tight or loose, flexible or inflexible. Some constraints turn out to be based on mere assumptions, and they end up having flexibility. Others are solid and binding, making the projects literally impossible. If you have an ironclad deadline that's six months more than you need, or an approaching deadline for which no one will worry if you miss it by a few months, it's a loose constraint. When the constraint is close and it has to be done just so, it's inflexible . . . and it's a headache.

There are various strategies for managing tight constraints, depending on each individual project's circumstances. Some constraints are nondiscretionary: they're simply facts. Managing nondiscretionary constraints requires creativity if the constraints are too tight. Straight-line solutions are closed off, but there may be ways to get around brick walls.

Some constraints are actually just preferences, as when your customer would sooner not spend the extra money but still wants it early. Preferences can be negotiated; the customer will likely prefer some trade-offs to others.

Other constraints are based on assumptions about what the customer wants and needs. Some assumptions are made by the customers, some by the project manager, some by other stakeholders. Assumptions first appear as nondiscretionary constraints or preferences, so probe every constraint to

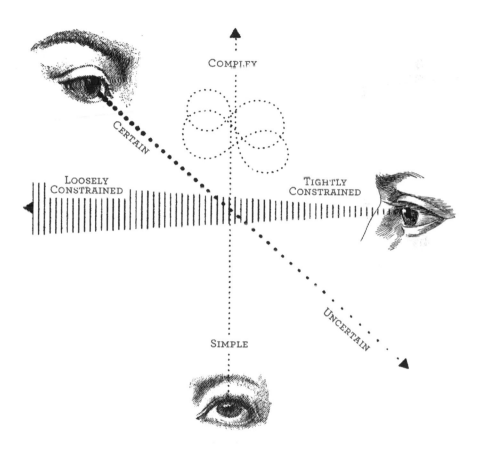

Figure 1-2. What makes a project hard? The three challenges are the tightness of the constraints, the complexity of the process, and the degree of certain knowledge about risks and issues.

make sure it isn't really an assumption. You may very well accept preferences or discretionary constraints as part of your project objective, but
it's vital to keep the difference clear in your own mind, especially when
trouble hits.

Complexity

There's no *theoretical* difference between a 10-line Gantt chart and a
10,000-line one, but there's an enormous *practical* difference. If there are
thousands of tasks, thousands of resources, or thousands of details, it
doesn't matter whether each individual one is easy. Complexity by itself
adds substantial challenge to any project.

Complexity comes in many forms, and a variety of disciplines exists
to help manage it. First on our list is classical project management
PMBOK style. By providing documented and controllable processes for
each step, formal project management provides tools to bring project
complexity to heel.

Another kind of complexity is technical. Systems engineering, for
example, exists to provide order, structure, and discipline in the sphere of
technical complexity. Logistics management helps tame the routing of
goods and services. Statistical process control and such tools as ISO-9000
certification ensure that manufacturing processes are repeatable and
consistent.

Gathering and analyzing information isn't free, of course, and the
tools are expensive. The cost/value ratio isn't linear. On small projects,
use of many tools is probably overkill. On huge projects, millions of planning dollars can salvage billions in performance dollars, making the cost/
value ratio extremely positive. But the blank space on the back of an envelope can be all the room you need to plan and manage a project as
simple as a trip to the grocery store.

Certainty

Former U.S. defense secretary Donald Rumsfeld in a 2002 press briefing
on the war in Iraq observed: "There are known knowns. These are things
we know that we know. There are known unknowns. That is to say, there
are things that we now know we don't know. But there are also unknown
unknowns. These are things we do not know we don't know." (As we'll

show later, Rumsfeld missed one: "unknown knowns"—the things we do not know that we really *do* know.)

Uncertainty is the third of our major project challenges. If your project involves mostly "known knowns" issues, certainty is high. The other categories involve unknowns, and unknowns create uncertainty.

We are not helpless in the face of uncertainty. We don't know whether it will rain on our company picnic, but knowing that we don't know empowers solutions ranging from renting tents to establishing alternate dates. We can make decisions with incomplete and unreliable data; we can think outside the box to develop solutions when none are immediately apparent; we can establish a reserve or make contingency plans to cope with the unexpected. There's a lot we can do about uncertainty, even if it can't be tamed altogether.

Uncertainty, by the way, is not identical to risk (i.e., the measure of potential threats and opportunities). As project managers know, risk (R) is defined as the probability (P) of an event happening times its impact (I) if it should happen: $R = P \times I$. This equation shapes the strategies and tactics you need to apply to achieve your objective, but while risk management helps manage uncertainty, it's usually not sufficient. Uncertainty takes us into the realm of Rumsfeld's "unknown unknowns." How do you perform risk management on a risk you don't even know exists in the first place? (We've got some tools for you later on in this book.)

Why We Get It Wrong

What aren't we seeing correctly—or at all?

In 1972, Nobel Prize winner Daniel Kahneman and MacArthur Fellow Amos Tversky identified the existence of systematic cognitive bias in the handling of risk. Cognitive biases are the filters and mental shortcuts we use to understand, predict, and make decisions about the world around us. The *availability heuristic* makes us think events are more likely when we can think of vivid examples: people often overestimate the likelihood of airplane crashes because they stick out in memory. *Egocentric bias* makes us think we're more responsible for a group action than other people would think. And there's the *illusion of transparency*, the idea that everyone knows how you feel—whether you've actually said anything or not. You'll learn about a number of these biases and blind spots through-out this book, and there's a section in the appendix with still more.

The most dangerous of them all is the *bias blind spot*—the bias of thinking we're less biased than other people. When we decide if someone else is biased, we observe his or her behavior. When we decide if we our-selves are biased, we look into our hearts and minds. It all *feels* right, so we assume we aren't biased.

Cognitive bias is at the heart of many failed projects. Customers often fail to see that many projects are like icebergs—90 percent of the work lies out of their field of vision. Project managers often see customer requirements as silly or self-destructive. Team members may see the proj-ect as ultimately foolish or doomed. Biases limit your creativity, and too often they make opportunities look like brick walls.

Testing for Cognitive Bias

You'll find taking this test of cognitive biases an interesting experience:

1. Is the sequence OXXXOXXXOXXOOOXOOXXOO random?
   a. Probably random
   b. Probably not random

2. Linda is 31 years old, single, outspoken, and very bright. She ma-jored in philosophy. As a student, she was deeply concerned with issues of discrimination and social justice, and she also participated in antinuclear demonstrations. Which of these statements is more probable?
   a. Linda is a bank teller.
   b. Linda is a bank teller and is active in the feminist movement.

3. You have an urn with 30 red balls and 60 other balls that are either black or yellow. You don't know the ratio of black to yellow, only that the total of black and yellow is 60. There is a prize for winning and no penalty for losing. Choose which wager you would prefer:
   a. You get $100 if you draw a red ball.
   b. You get $100 if you draw a black ball.

Now you get another draw with the same balls and the same rules, but you must choose one of the following wagers instead:

    c. You get $100 if you draw a red or a yellow ball.

    d. You get $100 if you draw a black or yellow ball.

4. In a city with 100 terrorists and one million nonterrorists, there is a special automated face recognition system that is 99 percent accurate. The alarm goes off, and trained Homeland Security agents swoop down. What is the probability their captive is really a terrorist?

    a. Very high (99 percent)

    b. High (over 75 percent)

    c. Moderate (between 25 percent and 75 percent)

    d. Low (under 25 percent)

    e. Very Low (under 1 percent)

5. Are English words that *begin* with the letters r or k (*roast, kale*) more common than English words that have r or k as the *third* letter (*street, acknowledge*)?

    a. Words that *begin* with r or k are much more common.

    b. Words that have r or k as their *third letter* are much more common.

    c. There are roughly the same number in each category.

6. We're preparing for an outbreak of a disease that's expected to kill 600 people. Of the following two strategies, which would you prefer?

    a. 200 people will be saved.

    b. There's a 1/3 probability 600 people will be saved, and a 2/3 probability no people will be saved.

As a backup strategy, you can also choose one of the following:

    c. 400 people will die.

    d. There's a 1/3 probability no one will die, and a 2/3 probability 600 people will die.

7. According to research, how much higher is the happiness rating of Californians compared to the happiness rating of Midwesterners?

    a. Californians have a much higher happiness rating than Midwesterners.

    b. Californians have a slightly higher happiness rating than Midwesterners.

    c. There is no difference in average happiness ratings.

    d. Midwesterners have a slightly higher happiness rating than Californians.

    e. Midwesterners have a much higher happiness rating than Californians.

Answers to Cognitive Bias Test

1. **Clustering illusion.** If you think the sequence looks nonrandom, you're with the majority—but you're wrong. The sequence has several characteristics of a random sequence, such as an equal number of each result and an equal number of adjacent results. But people seem to expect a "random" sequence to have a greater number of alternations (O to X, or vice versa) than statistics would predict. The chance of an alternation in a sequence of independent random binary events (flips of heads or tails) is 50 percent, but people seem to expect an alternation rate of about 70 percent. This creates a "clustering illusion," in which ostensibly meaningful streaks and patterns appear in random data.

2. **Conjunction fallacy.** If you answered (b), 85 percent of people agree with you—but again, you're wrong. The probability of two events occurring together is always less than or equal to the probability of either one occurring alone. Even if there's a very low probability Linda is a bank teller (let's make it 5 percent) and a very high probability that Linda is active in the feminist movement (say, 95 percent), the chance that Linda is a bank teller *and* active in the feminist movement is 5 percent × 95 percent, or 4.75 percent, which is lower than the chance of her being a bank teller alone. The conjunction fallacy leads us to believe that a very specific scenario is more probable than a more general one, but logic tells us that can never be the case.

3. **Ambiguity aversion effect.** Which pair did you choose? If you prefer gamble (a) to gamble (b), logically, you should also prefer gamble (c) to gamble (d); the number of yellow balls is the same. If you prefer

gamble (b) to gamble (a), by similar logic you should prefer gamble (d) to gamble (c). But in actual surveys, most people strictly prefer gamble (a) to gamble (b), and gamble (d) to gamble (c). The logic that informs one decision breaks down for the other.

The idea of the ambiguity effect is that people prefer known risks over unknown risks, regardless of other factors. Choosing gamble (a) over gamble (b) is a preference for knowing the number of red balls, even though the number of black balls might be greater. Choosing gamble (d) over gamble (c) is a preference for knowing that the sum of black and yellow balls is 60, even if the sum of red and yellow might be greater.

4. **Base rate fallacy.** The correct answer is (e), or 0.98 percent. The base rate fallacy occurs when you don't notice that the *failure rate* (1 in 100) is the not the same as the *false alarm rate*. The false alarm rate is completely different, because there are, after all, far more nonterrorists than terrorists. Let's imagine that we walk everyone—100 terrorists and 1,000,000 nonterrorists, for a total of 1,000,100 people—in front of the face recognition tool. A 1 percent failure rate means it's going to ring incorrectly one time for each 100 passengers, 10,099 times in total. It will catch 99 terrorists and miss 1, but it's also going to catch 10,000 nonterrorists. The ratio is actually 99/10,099, or a miniscule 0.98 percent, that the person caught is actually a terrorist.

5. **Availability heuristic.** There are roughly three times as many English words with *r* or *k* as the third letter than there are words that begin with *r* or *k*. However, it's easier to think of words in the first group than words in the second group. The availability heuristic leads us to believe that what is easy to recall is also more probable, when in this case the opposite is true.

6. **Framing effect.** Which pair did you choose? In a 1981 study, Tversky and Kahneman presented this problem to two different groups. One got the first two choices; the other got the second pair. In the first, 72 percent preferred (a). In the second, 78 percent preferred (d).

Mathematically, (a) and (c) are identical, as are (b) and (d). If you chose (a) and (d) [or (b) and (c)], you responded to the same information in an opposite manner based on whether the positive or negative spin was presented.

7. **Focalism.** The correct answer is (c); there is no significant difference. Focalism is the tendency to overrely on a single piece of information. Most people choose (a) or (b), and when asked why, people overvalued the effect of sunshine, and accordingly undervalued other factors that also have a large impact on net happiness. (If you chose the Midwest for happiness, it's the same cognitive bias, just reversed.)

You may have done very well, or maybe not so well, on this test. If you didn't do so well, it may be worth spending some time training yourself to recognize when you're falling into one of these cognitive traps.

If you did do well, it's not because you don't have the same tendencies as the rest of us but because you've already trained yourself to correct for at least some of those biases. You can tell that your unconscious mind wants to go immediately to the wrong choice; it's your conscious analysis that helps you find the right answer.

We're all biased, but there's a big difference between the person who challenges his or her own thought processes and the person who ignores or even embraces the bias and charges blindly into that good night. Challenging ourselves and our own thinking is vital to managing our projects to a successful conclusion.

To Uncertainty . . . and Beyond!

In our work with thousands of project managers across many fields in diverse industries and specialties ranging from IT to marketing, we've had the opportunity to hear firsthand many of the difficulties people in the trenches deal with every day. We've learned the stories behind some of the most amazing horrors circulating in today's project management literature. What's interesting to us is not the variety of causes and symptoms in these stories but rather their similarities: assumptions that didn't pan out, customers who didn't communicate, plans that weren't made. It isn't "one blasted thing after another," it's usually the same blasted thing over and over again. And yet, the fundamental lesson seldom gets learned. For all project management's worthy emphasis on the vital necessity of "lessons learned," too often the lessons aren't recognized in the first place, much less learned. (We've got some advice in Chapter 10 that can help.)

Limited resources, competing priorities, and too little control are not limited to the profession of project management. Hardly anyone who works for a living does not recognize these pressures. What complicates project management in particular is the degree of uncertainty, the extent to which key information is unavailable, unreliable, or even unknowable. To prosper, project managers don't just need the traditional tools of their profession; they need to know the right way to *think* about the job at hand.

When work is "temporary and unique," the unique part guarantees the presence of uncertainty. A project is a means to an end. It's not undertaken for its own sake; rather, it's done to achieve a goal that somebody finds worthwhile enough to pay for it. The first place a project can go off the rails is at the very beginning, if customers do not see their own objectives clearly or if their best guess as to how to solve the problem turns out not to work. And that's only the beginning.

We have both spent our careers studying the operational art of thinking: the right thoughts, on time, on schedule, and to spec. Sometimes that overlaps with creativity. Other times, it's more concerned with decision making. And most important, it's concerned with effective management of and response to risk.

In this book, we describe a specific, operational process to help you manage the ambiguity, uncertainty, risk, and speed of change on projects. We call it "creative project management," and we mean creative in a broad sense: a mindset primed to recognize opportunity, find answers to problems, and gain insights into process and methodology to make today's and tomorrow's projects better and better.

The first part of the creative process is identifying the key question. The second part is to find the optimal answer. Most books on creativity start there. But there's a third part, and project managers all know it: the planning and follow-through that turns a good idea into a real solution. Project managers tend to be great in planning and follow-through, good in coming up with creative ideas, and not so good in asking the right questions. Without asking the right question, you're going to have a lot of trouble finding the right answer.

In performing "lessons learned" analyses, which we will describe in Chapter 10, we've observed that there is always a question that, if asked early enough, would have identified the biggest problems that faced the project. Whether the question was asked or not, of course, is something completely different. But certain questions tended to show up more frequently in after-action reports than others.

Some of what we have to say can be taken as criticism of the people or companies whose stories we tell, but that's not our intent. These people have substantial merit, or else they wouldn't have ended up in positions of leadership. We do not pretend to have any special knowledge of the innermost thoughts of leaders who have either presided over disasters or presided over their avoidance. To our eyes, the purpose of "lessons learned," the necessary end to any well-run project, is not to find fault or even praise but to find tools to help us do better in the future.

There are, after all, two ways of learning: (1) have an experience and learn from it, and (2) find someone else who's had an experience and learn from him or her. The second method is often cheaper. We assume that most readers already have a command of the basic vocabulary of tools of project management. If you don't, don't worry. On our blog at www .sidewisethinking.blogspot.com we've provided all the necessary details, including a reading list, so that you can read more about it.

2

What We Know and What We Think

The most erroneous stories are those we think we know best—
and therefore never scrutinize or question.
—Stephen Jay Gould, naturalist and author, *Full House*, 1997

Where's Your Blind Spot?

There's a difference between what we know and what we think we know, but sometimes it's hard to be sure. Assumptions, that key PMBOK concept, are what we think we know. Project managers are supposed to challenge assumptions whenever possible. That's easier said than done, though. Every one of us has blind spots—cognitive biases and perceptual errors that keep us from recognizing our own misjudgments. To be an effective manager of any stripe, and especially a project manager, you have to manage your blind spots. Doing so is every bit as challenging as it sounds. Some blind spots you don't know you have; some you know about and work on actively; and others you just surrender to (or embrace).

Even when we recognize our blind spots, too often we stop at mere awareness. It is important to understand that managing or addressing our individual cognitive biases is different from being aware of our shortcomings.

Someone might say, for instance, "Yes, I know I'm a micromanager, but that's just the way I am." That person is aware of a blind spot, and may even be aware that it's a problem, but doesn't show any motivation to deal with it. The micromanager who says, "I'm taking a workshop to improve my delegation skills, and I'm working with an executive coach" may still be micromanaging today, but there's clearly a good-faith effort to do better.

On the other hand, a micromanager who says, "Absolutely, I micromanage, and I have to! Those incompetents couldn't spell their own names if I didn't check them!" embraces the problem and regards it as a virtue.

The underlying motives can be complex. Perhaps the micromanager secretly enjoys the behavior, because he or she is rewarded for it in some way, or—surprisingly often—because the micromanager doesn't know how to fix the habit or what to replace it with.

Let's look at some proactive strategies for managing your blind spots.

Compensating

The original "blind spot" is physiological: the one in your eye where the optic nerve passes through the optic disc. There aren't any light-detecting cells in this area, so your field of vision has a small void that the brain normally compensates for to produce clear vision. You can see the effect in Figure 2-1.

In the field of management, some blind spots tend to be inherent in much the same way. You don't usually have detailed daily knowledge of what your competition is up to or what next quarter's stock market is going to look like. These kinds of blind spots, like the physiological one, can't be solved. You have to compensate for them.

Figure 2-1. To find your physiological blind spot, get close to the page, close your right eye, and stare at the star. Now slowly move the book away. As you move it away, at some point, the circle will disappear; farther away it will reappear. The area in which you cannot see the star is your blind spot.

In the case of our physiological blind spot, let's look at the options.

If you can't see the circle from one perspective, changing the perspective (moving the book to a different position) makes it visible. You also can infer the circle's existence from the caption under the figure. If you've seen the figure elsewhere, you can make an intelligent guess about it merely by knowing the subject. If you tend to make the same error repeatedly, you can double-check yourself or get someone else to check it for you.

What you don't want to do is fall for the optical illusion your brain provides when it fills in the blind spot for you

Scanning

When driving a vehicle, your blind spot is the area you can't observe directly under existing circumstances (see Figure 2-2). When you are looking forward, you create blind spots in the rear and sides. If you turn your head or glance in the side mirror or rearview mirror, you can eliminate one blind spot, but you create another when you do so. In this situation, the strategy is clear: scanning. No one can take in all points of view simultaneously. Drivers routinely shift their eyes from one field of vision to another, especially when contemplating a change in direction or speed.

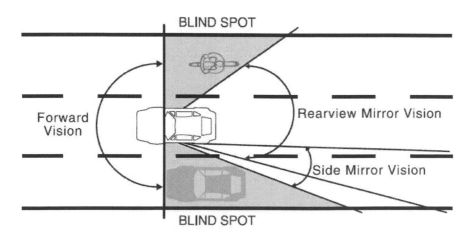

Figure 2-2. An automobile driver's blind spot is the area that can't be seen through forward vision or mirrors without turning the head.

Similarly, for project managers, shifting points of view or areas of focus help correct for many different kinds of blind spots on projects to respond to a changing environment. Scanning your environment means looking from many points of view one at a time, but doing so quickly. Such strategies as management by walking around (MBWA) and brainstorming sessions aimed at improvement rather than problem solving can help you scan your project environment.

Listening

Blind spots in interpersonal relationships are especially tricky for project managers for two reasons. First, a lot of project managers come from tech-

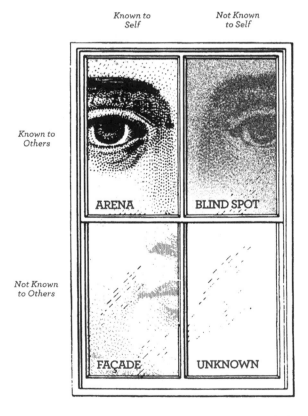

Figure 2-3. The Johari window helps identify blinds spots in interpersonal communication and relationships.

nical ranks in which intellect and reason tend to dominate emotion. Second, project managers typically have weak formal power and must gain the cooperation of people who do not report to them. Like Tennessee Williams's character Blanche DuBois, project managers all too often must "depend on the kindness of strangers." Unlike Blanche, many project managers don't have the charm to do so.

Fortunately, there are several tools you can use to illuminate the differences between how you see yourself and how others may see you. The Johari window (see Figure 2-3) is a psychological tool created in the 1950s that is very useful in this regard. The different perspectives it reveals can be a powerful tool to understand your blind spot(s) and improve performance.

In the Johari window exercise, you select five or six adjectives from the list shown in Table 2-1 that you think describe your own personality. Next, you ask people you know and respect from your place of business to each pick five or six words from the list that *they* think describe your personality.

Table 2-1. Johari Adjectives

able	accepting	adaptable	bold
brave	calm	caring	cheerful
clever	complex	confident	dependable
dignified	energetic	extroverted	friendly
giving	happy	helpful	idealistic
independent	ingenious	intelligent	introverted
kind	knowledgeable	logical	loving
mature	modest	nervous	observant
organized	patient	powerful	proud
quiet	reflective	relaxed	religious
responsive	searching	self-assertive	self-conscious
sensible	sentimental	shy	silly
smart	spontaneous	sympathetic	tense
trustworthy	warm	wise	witty

Once you've collected the feedback, sort the words into the four quadrants of the grid using the standards in Table 2-2.

Table 2-2. The Johari Window Quadrant

Quadrant	What Goes In It	What It Reveals
Arena	Words chosen by both you and those you know	Your public self
Façade	Words chosen by you but not by those you know	What you conceal from others
Blind Spot	Words chosen by those you know but not by you	The conflict between how you see yourself and how others see you
Unknown	No one chose those words to describe you	Maybe they don't apply; maybe no one knows what's in your secret heart—not even you

To learn from the Johari window, you have to respect and pay attention to the feedback from your closest associates. How do they see you? How does your behavior affect the behavior of other people? What do they want and need from you, and will this in turn influence them to do what you require? They may not always be right, but their perspective is still invaluable. How people see you determines how they'll act toward you.

In addition to listening to the feedback people give you in the Johari window, you should also always be listening to your colleagues for clues about your blind spots. Effective listening is more than just something you do with your ears; it's something you do with all five of your senses. Psychologist Albert Mehrabian's famous communications model found that only 7 percent of communication is based on words. Listeners form far more of their beliefs and opinions about your message based on your tone of voice (38 percent) and facial expressions (55 percent). Professor Mehrabian's study illustrates that a stunning 93 percent of communications is based not on the spoken word but on the method of delivery. This creates a communications blind spot with significant implications for project performance. Learn to speak with the understanding that recipients are using all five senses to listen. Equally important, pay attention not only to what people *say* but, more important, to what they *don't* say.

Learning

The Project Management Institute has a standard for professional responsibility among project managers, setting forth laudable goals in the areas of respect, fairness, and honesty.

To us, one of the foremost standards of professional responsibility for project management practitioners is the commitment to *lessons learned.* The PMBOK, and indeed every other project management process of which we're aware, endorses lessons learned as the mandatory final stage of any project life cycle.

Lessons learned, however, are frequently limited to project performance and not to self-evaluation. A project team's lessons learned review generally seeks to identify what went wrong or right (and too often focuses on who's to blame) rather than focusing on human factors, process, and opportunities for improvement on future projects. Consider conducting a lessons learned on your history as a project manager to discover what kinds of blind spots you might have and how they might affect project performance. A questioning mindset is the most powerful tool to combat mental blind spots.

Three More Essential Project Questions

In our first chapter, we identified four questions that accounted for the most common causes of project failure. We've added a few more to the list:

- Why are we doing this?

- Who has an interest in what we're doing, and what do they each want and need?

- What do we have to do, and how are we going to do it?

- Who needs to be involved, and in what way?

- What makes this project hard?

- What aren't we seeing correctly—or at all?

- How will people react to this project?

- What if I'm wrong?

- What am I not seeing?

We'll continue adding to this list throughout the book. For the complete list of questions, see "Questions for the Questioning Project Manager," in the appendix.

How Will People React to This Project?

Fish, it is said, do not notice water, and we humans seldom notice air. Project managers have a similar tendency to downplay the management of the environment in which the project takes place in favor of managing the details of the project itself. This lack of attention paid to the project environment can lead to catastrophe, as it did in the case of Dr. Ignaz Semmelweis (see Figure 2-4).

Semmelweis, assistant to the head of obstetrics at the Vienna General Hospital in the 1840s, noticed a troubling fact. His clinic, where doctors were trained, had a maternal mortality rate from puerperal fever that averaged 10 percent. A second clinic, which trained midwives, had a mortality rate of only 4 percent.

This unfortunate disparity was well known outside the hospital. Semmelweis described women begging on their knees to go to the midwives clinic rather than risk the care of doctors. This situation, Semmelweis said, "made me so miserable that life seemed worthless." Semmelweis started a systematic analysis to find out the cause, ruling out overcrowding, climate, and other factors before an accident pointed the way to a solution. His good friend Jakob Kolletschka died from a condition similar

Figure 2-4. Ignaz Semmelweis, who discovered the importance of hand washing in preventing disease, also helped name the Semmelweis reflex, a type of cognitive bias.

to puerperal fever after being accidentally cut with a student's scalpel during an autopsy.

Because the germ theory of disease was unknown at that time, Semmelweis thought that some sort of "cadaverous particles" might be responsible. Midwives, after all, didn't perform autopsies, and so they were not exposed to the same bacteria. Accordingly, Semmelweis required doctors to wash their hands in a mild bleach solution after performing autopsies. Following the change in procedures, death rates in the doctor's clinic dropped almost immediately to the levels of the midwives' clinic.

This theory contradicted medical belief of the time, and Semmelweis eventually was disgraced, lost his job, and began accusing his fellow physicians of murder. His career—and sanity—deteriorated steadily, and some years later Semmelweis eventually died in a mental institution, possibly after being beaten by a guard.

In addition to his medical research, which helped inspire Louis Pasteur's development of the germ theory of disease, Semmelweis indirectly helped identify an important bias that continues to affect our cognitive processes: the Semmelweis reflex. Credited to author Robert Anton Wilson, the Semmelweis reflex is "the automatic rejection of the obvious, without thought, inspection, or experiment." But that only defines the term without explaining it. What happened here?

Let's apply the first four of our essential project questions to Dr. Semmelweis (see Table 2-3).

Table 2-3. Essential Project Questions for Ignaz Semmelweis

Question	Answers
Why are we doing this?	To save lives and improve medical practice
Who has an interest in what we're doing, and what do they each want and need?	Patients—Need to avoid disease or receive cure Physicians—Want to save lives, need information and training Professional community—Need proper scientific evidence
What do we have to do, and how are we going to do it?	Scientific—Develop hypothesis, conduct tests, analyze data, prepare reports, obtain peer review and publication, present findings to fellow physicians Outreach—Provide education and information to get physicians to adopt the new technique
Who needs to be involved, and in what way?	Project team—do the work Hospital and colleagues—support the work Medical community—accept and implement the conclusions

At first glance, the problem seems to lie squarely in the scientific and technical area of the project. We design an experiment, we perform an experiment, and we learn from the experiment. If we're fortunate enough to come up with a workable answer, then other scientists can replicate our work, confirming the result. Once convinced of the outcome, they'll naturally want to adopt the new procedures.

Like most project managers, Semmelweis thought managing the project was his chief function, and he did his job well, coming up with a creative solution that could save the lives of thousands of women. Ultimately, Semmelweis failed. Pasteur finished the research and solved the problem. The trouble is, Semmelweis could have made it happen if his project management and environmental management skills had been of the same quality as his scientific and medical skills. Where he failed was in managing the environment around him. Let's see how assumptions and cognitive biases played into the problem, starting with the one that bears his name.

Semmelweis Reflex

If Semmelweis's hypothesis about hand washing is correct, the impact is far reaching. It means that physicians will have to acknowledge that their own behavior has contributed to the deaths of thousands of patients. Who wants to think of himself or herself as a killer, however inadvertent? The Semmelweis reflex is better stated as the human tendency to reject or challenge information that portrays us in a negative light.

Semmelweis started gently, by laying out his research in a traditional fashion. He must have been shocked at the level of instant rejection by his peers. Why would doctors reject an idea that had the possibility of saving so many lives? In this case, the other doctors could only accept or deny the results—and the results showed that they had been contributing to people's deaths.

Semmelweis's response assumed the problem was that doctors were *unaware* of their responsibility, so his logical next step was to call them murderers for refusing to take the necessary steps to stop the deaths. But that, as you can see, could only make things worse. The positions of Semmelweis's colleagues hardened as he insisted more adamantly on his theory's validity. It would take a generation for the germ theory to take hold.

So, when you're accused of fault in the course of completing a project, watch for the Semmelweis reflex in yourself. The natural first impulse is to deny or deflect, but the right practice is to examine and explore. Depending on what you find, you can select a more reasoned strategy.

Belief Bias

How did the contemporaries of Dr. Semmelweis manage to deny the evidence? The supporting evidence was all there for inspection, and the results clearly demonstrated improved survival rates. Actually, it's fairly easy:

if you're sure someone's conclusion is wrong, there's obviously some problem with the data or the process. A lot of the debate about global warming is distorted by belief bias.

We should add that if your immediate reaction on reading those words is to agree that, yes, the other side's opinions *are* distorted by belief bias, take that as a none-too-gentle hint that your own belief bias may be operating here as well.

Belief bias is the tendency for all of us to evaluate the logical strength of someone's argument based on whether we believe in the truth or falsity of the conclusion. In everyday life, it's why it's so hard for our logical, well-reasoned arguments to penetrate other people's thick skulls. And, of course, it's also the reason people so seldom give logical, well-reasoned arguments to support their idiotic ideas.

The Red Queen in Lewis Carroll's classic *Through the Looking-Glass* practiced believing five impossible things before breakfast. We agree with this strategy (to a certain extent). Several leading business coaches also strongly recommend thoroughly studying topics or issues that you disagree with or don't understand to gain new perspectives as part of ongoing individual development. Make sure you look at a diversity of information and spend effort imagining how a reasonable person could reach a conclusion so different from your own. This isn't necessarily an argument for you to change your beliefs; instead, it's strong encouragement to make sure your beliefs don't suffer from hardening of the mental arteries.

Confirmation Bias

In a 1979 study of a group of people (half of whom strongly supported capital punishment and half of whom strongly opposed it), each participant was given quick descriptions of two studies. One study gave evidence that the death penalty was effective; the other argued that it was ineffective. Results of the study demonstrated that, regardless of the participants' original opinion, each group tended to shift slightly in the direction of the first study they read.

If you're being presented with new information that may change an opinion you already hold, you tend to demand a higher standard of proof. That's not inherently unreasonable, but it is a bias.

If you suspect that you're falling into confirmation bias, the first thing to do is to establish your own threshold of proof. Specifically, ask yourself, "What specific evidence, if found, would prove to me that I am wrong?"

That leads us to the next essential project question.

What If I'm Wrong?

In April 1944, Sewell L. Avery, chairman of giant retailer Montgomery Ward, was forcibly carried out of his office for refusing to obey an order of the National War Labor Board. Confronting Attorney General Francis Biddle, who was personally supervising the military seizure and occupation of Montgomery Ward corporate offices, Avery shouted, "To hell with the government, you . . . you . . . New Dealer!"

President Franklin D. Roosevelt, on vacation in South Carolina, was reportedly "vastly entertained" by the resultant photograph of the defiant Avery, arms crossed, being supported by two struggling soldiers.

Sewell Avery (see Figure 2-5) was a "definite" kind of man, you might

Figure 2-5. Sewell Avery being removed from his office by National Guardsmen, April 27, 1944, for refusing to obey orders of the National War Labor Board.

say. Born into a wealthy, prominent family in the Michigan lumber industry, he received his degree from the University of Michigan Law School and eventually became president of U.S. Gypsum. Early in his career Avery established a strong track record as a capable and energetic leader, with a particular knack for cost cutting. His skills are credited with U.S. Gypsum remaining profitable during the entire Great Depression.

Montgomery Ward had done less well, suffering from the general collapse of retailing nationwide. The company's banker, J. P. Morgan & Company, decided that Montgomery Ward, struggling with growing debt, needed a change in leadership. The board elected to reach outside the retailing world for someone with an established record who knew how to manage in bad times. That man was Sewell Avery.

He was a capable executive with strong project management skills. While keeping his old job as president of U.S. Gypsum, Avery turned around Montgomery Ward, from a 1931 loss of $8.7 million ($122 million in 2008 dollars) to a profit of $2 million (current equivalent: $32 million) in 1934. He was a tough taskmaster. Four company presidents and 30 vice presidents resigned or were fired in Avery's first decade as Montgomery Ward chairman. (The running joke was that his name was S. L. Avery, and that's why working for him resembled slavery.)

In 1939 the U.S. economy was showing sign of improvement, and Montgomery Ward began expanding in city centers even as American involvement in the war overseas became increasingly probable. Table 2-4 shows how Montgomery Ward stacked up against its major competitors, Sears and JCPenney.

Table 2-4. Comparison of Major Retail Chains

Chain	1938	Comments
Montgomery Ward	600 stores; $400 million sales	Founded 1872; first large mail-order business; first "outlet" stores in 1921
Sears	496 stores; $500 million sales	Founded 1888; first retail stores in 1925
JCPenney	1,500 stores; $250 million sales	Founded 1912, in Longmont, Colorado

World War II caused a retrenchment in the plans of all the major retail chains, but Sewell Avery had a plan, based on his experience at U.S. Gypsum. He knew what would happen when the war ended, because he'd seen it before. A temporary burst of economic activity from pent-up consumer demand inevitably led to an inflationary bubble followed by a new market crash.

The United States, Avery was sure, would experience major difficulties moving from a wartime economy to a peacetime one. Millions of troops would return, all seeking jobs. At the same time, factories geared for the production of tanks, bombers, and fighting ships would grind to a halt as the need for their wartime production ceased.

Avery was not alone in his belief. Many leading economists also predicted that the United States would fall back into the Great Depression. The massive financial stimulus provided by World War II would dramatically wind down just as millions of veterans would come home to seek nonexistent jobs, and the nation would return to *status quo ante*.

Let Sears and JCPenney expand, the thinking went; Montgomery Ward would stand pat on its massive cash reserves (one Ward vice president famously said, "Wards is one of the finest banks with a storefront in the U.S. today"), and when the inevitable collapse came, Montgomery Ward would swallow its rivals at pennies on the dollar.

As we know, it didn't turn out that way. Instead of falling back into depression, the United States in the postwar years saw unprecedented economic growth.

Sewell Avery was, obviously, wrong. But was he also irrational?

Known, Unknown, and Uncertain

It was once said of Vietnam, "Anybody who thinks he knows what's going on clearly doesn't understand the situation." As we key in these words in late 2009, any number of predictions about the near-term economic future are making the rounds. From your vantage point as reader, our future is your past. You know which predictions worked out, and which did not. If we had your knowledge today, we could make an awful lot of money. But, alas, that's not the way it works.

Sewell Avery's circumstances were very much like our own. Just because we don't know what's going on doesn't mean we aren't required to make a decision. The outcome of the decision doesn't by itself prove whether the decision was good or bad—lottery tickets are a bad investment, but sometimes people win; seat belts save lives except in certain accidents.

In 1945, no one knew for sure what the postwar world would be like. To understand the future, the only resource we have is the past. It was certainly not unreasonable to conclude that a nation traumatized by depression might well fall back into one.

But it was far from certain.

Year after year the economy grew, but Avery stuck to his guns and refused to permit expansion, expecting the Depression to return any minute. Sears and JCPenney grew in size and in profits (see Figures 2-6 and 2-7), and by 1954 Montgomery Ward was a lagging also-ran in the department store business, a position from which it never recovered. Eventually the chain declared bankruptcy and closed in 2001, though it's since been revived as an online retailer.

A defensible decision in 1946 isn't necessarily defensible in 1954. It's obvious—especially from our lofty position in the all-knowing future—that Avery should have behaved differently. He could have established

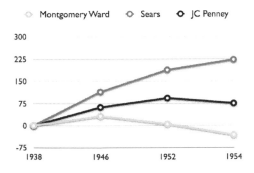

Number of Stores

Figure 2-6. Change in number of stores operated by Montgomery Ward, Sears, and JCPenney, 1938–1954.

metrics to monitor his assumptions, identified signposts or early warning signals that might sharpen the accuracy and confirm his predictions, or hedged his strategy by opening at least a few new stores.

By implication, criticizing Avery means praising the leadership of Sears, but what if the economy had swung the other way? Sears invested about $500 million (the rough equivalent of $7.5 billion in 2009 dollars) in its mammoth postwar expansion, but it didn't spend it all in a single year. If the economy did return to prewar depression or even slower growth, it's hard to believe Sears would not have curtailed or modified its spending.

Sewell Avery was clearly not a stupid man. Such a man would never have risen to the chairmanship of U.S. Gypsum or a chain like Montgomery Ward in the first place. And that makes this example all the more interesting. We too have reasons to believe in our intelligence, judgment, and track record. When a man like Sewell Avery makes a mistake that in hindsight seems so obvious and so easily avoided, there's something going on, something to learn.

We believe Avery's problem can be traced to undetected and unchallenged cognitive biases.

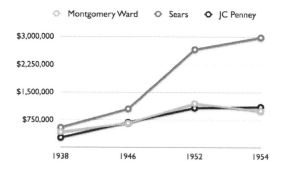

Figure 2-7. Sales growth (in $000) of Montgomery Ward, Sears, and JCPenney, 1938–1954.

Confirmation Bias

We tend to overvalue information if it supports our perceptions or hypotheses. During the period from 1945 to 1954, Montgomery Ward sales increased by 241 percent. Avery had every reason to feel that his judgment was vindicated.

In a vacuum, 241 percent growth looks great, but it's a number without a context. JCPenney grew 429 percent in that same period, moving from a distant third place to pull ahead of Montgomery Ward in total sales. Sears grew a whopping 555 percent, selling more than its two main rivals combined.

The confirmation bias involves selectively collecting and interpreting information that reinforces our ideas. The information we collect may be accurate; it's just incomplete. The way in which that information reinforces itself leads to another error: overconfidence.

Overconfidence (The Lake Wobegon Effect)

In Garrison Keillor's imaginary town of Lake Wobegon, Minnesota, "all the women are strong, all the men are good looking, and all the children are above average." While that's a joke, we laugh precisely because we know we think the same way. We tend to overestimate our good qualities and underestimate our bad ones. In a 1976 study, a million SAT-taking students rated themselves on their positive characteristics. For leadership ability, 70 percent put themselves in the top 50 percent. When it came to working and playing well with others, 85 percent thought they were in the upper half, and fully 25 percent thought they were in the top 1 percent. When people rate their decisions as being "95 percent certain," research shows they're wrong about 40 percent of the time. Sewell Avery was at least 95 percent certain of his own correctness. He should have allowed for a 40 percent chance he was wrong.

Primacy Effect

We've established that Avery's initial postwar decision was far from irrational and may have been arguably prudent. However, as the postwar economic boom gathered steam, Avery did not see that his idea was flawed, in spite of increasing data that showed continuing economic growth.

The primacy effect is the tendency to weigh the first effect or piece of information more heavily than information received subsequently. Once Avery internalized the idea that the Great Depression would ultimately return, he could always find some reasonably relevant data to support his opinion. Subsequent contradictory economic data was simply a temporary aberration. The crash was due at any moment.

What Am I Not Seeing?

While Sewell Avery was predicting economic disaster as soon as the stimulus package known as World War II came to an end, Allied generals fighting in the European Theater of Operations were looking at a different kind of disaster. There's a famous scene in the movie *Patton* that reflects the complex and dangerous situation they faced.

The Germans had just launched Operation Wacht am Rhein, better known as the Battle of the Bulge. Three entire armies, led by the First SS Panzer Division *Leibstandarte Adolf Hitler,* were attacking through the supposedly impenetrable Ardennes Forest. It was a devastating surprise to the Allied High Command.

Elements of the First U.S. Army, supposedly in a quiet sector of the front, were pinned down in Bastogne, a small village in Belgium. British Field Marshal Bernard Montgomery required weeks before his troops could possibly relieve the beleaguered American forces.

Allied supreme commander General Dwight Eisenhower asked Third Army Commander General George Patton, "How long will it take you to get Third Army moving north?"

"I can attack with two divisions in 48 hours," Patton replied, to a round of snickering from the other senior generals present.

Patton's boss, General Omar Bradley, was not amused. "Ike wants a realistic estimate, George. You're in the middle of a fight now. It's over a hundred miles to Bastogne."

But in the next scene, troops are marching to rescue the battered Allied 101st Airborne.

The assembled generals were right to be skeptical. Extricating three divisions from a fight and moving them 100 miles in 48 hours? Impossible!

Let's take a look at what is involved.

A division is an Army unit consisting of approximately 15,000 soldiers, along with everything they need to do their job. Imagine picking up a town of 45,000 (three divisions), with all the logistics services needed to keep them going, and moving 100 miles in 48 hours. For starters, if you don't have a detailed traffic movement plan, you'll end up with the world's biggest traffic jam. Armored vehicles are gas guzzlers, soldiers have to eat, and soldiers need ammunition. That means you'll have to preposition gas, food, and supplies along the route. A moving division is more vulnerable than a stationary force with established defense. That means you need fighting units to protect moving units, and they need more gas and food and ammunition.

A move of this nature requires a planning staff in the hundreds. In World War II, without cell phones, laptop computers, and Global Positioning Systems (GPS), orders were typed on mimeograph stencils, duplicated, and hand-carried to unit commanders stretched out over an immense area. Today's technology is far superior, but so are the demands involved.

It takes weeks to pull off an operation of this size and complexity. It can't possibly be done in 48 hours.

And yet it was.

As with any good magic trick, it's interesting to learn just how the apparently impossible happened. In this case, Patton anticipated the German offensive coming; therefore, he knew forces would have to move quickly to respond. He had his staff hard at work preparing the necessary orders for three different contingency plans well in advance of the Allied command fateful meeting.

Patton was the only senior American commander to anticipate correctly the German assault. Strangely, he was helped by something we wouldn't normally consider helpful—insufficient information. He was not cleared for Ultra, the highly classified project that had broken the top-secret Enigma cipher used by the German high command. Along the Western front, however, the Germans weren't transmitting messages coded with Enigma; for the most part, units were close enough together to have in-person planning sessions. Radio traffic was restricted, resulting in an increased sense that all was quiet on the Western front. A lack of Enigma messages and decreased radio traffic confirmed the Allied High Command's cognitive bias that the war was in its final stages. No one except Patton was looking for problems.

Patton, however, remembering that the Germans had already come through the impenetrable Ardennes twice (once in World War I and again earlier in World War II), both times with disastrous results for their enemies, viewed the battlefield from a different perspective. He had his intelligence staff looking closely at the area, and he found evidence of a buildup.

The difference between possible and impossible can be just a function of the time constraint. When we say "nothing is impossible," as noted earlier, we usually envision a universe of unlimited time, unlimited resources, and really flexible performance standards. But that's not the real world. When we're asked to do something, we have to do it within the boundaries of the triple constraints of time, cost, and performance. Magicians plan well in advance. Often, by the time you know a trick is about to start, it's already over. You're just waiting for the reveal.

When Patton left the meeting with Eisenhower, Bradley, Montgomery, and the others, he went down to his jeep, picked up the radio, contacted his headquarters, and issued a one-word code ("Pickle") to implement the appropriate preexisting plan.

Patton's driver, Sergeant John Mims, reportedly said, "I don't know why they need all them other generals. You and me can run this whole war out of your jeep."

George Patton saw what the assembled Allied headquarters intelligence operation did not, and yet the same tools were available to everyone. (The intelligence staff, in fact, probably had superior tools.) It's not that Patton wasn't subject to cognitive bias—we all are. It's how you manage those biases that counts.

Anchoring Bias

The anchoring bias occurs when you rely too heavily on a single aspect of a situation to make your decision. Doing so forces you to undervalue other aspects of the situation. Too much reliance on the Ultra code intercepts created an anchor that in turn caused other intelligence information to be discounted.

Patton also demonstrated some anchoring bias of his own. A keen student of history, he focused on the Ardennes Forest area precisely because the Germans had invaded that way twice before. He may well have downplayed other evidence in favor of a more detailed look at that sector, which was not even in his area.

If Patton's behavior was also the result of a cognitive bias, then what's the difference between Patton and the intelligence officers who didn't see the German offensive coming? First, the difference is that Patton didn't merely assume the Germans were coming and plan accordingly; he looked for evidence. It's more difficult to look for evidence that you're wrong than evidence that you're right, but that's what distinguishes a winning general or project manager.

Astute project managers understand that the project environment is fluid. They have a willingness to question their own assumptions and beliefs, and they often actively seek evidence in those areas.

Herd Instinct

The herd instinct tells us to keep our heads down and join the majority to improve our safety and comfort. If the intelligence community as a whole doesn't think there's a problem, the burden of proof lies on the shoulders of those who do—unless those shoulders carry three stars, as did George Patton's.

Like all cognitive biases, there's justification. The Japanese say, "The nail that sticks up gets hammered down." It's hard not to follow the crowd. Besides, the crowd may be right.

Some people are rebellious by nature; they push back against the herd instinct just as reflexively as others follow, and that's a problem as well. As noted astrophysicist Carl Sagan once observed: "The fact that some geniuses were laughed at does not imply that all who are laughed at are geniuses. They laughed at Columbus, they laughed at Fulton, they laughed at the Wright brothers. But they also laughed at Bozo the Clown."

The problem isn't following the crowd; it's following the crowd *mindlessly*. What if the crowd is wrong? How would you know? For example: if you were an Ultra-cleared intelligence officer, what could you ask yourself to challenge your thinking bias?

- Am I relying too much on one source of information?

■ What other sources of information are available to corroborate my conclusions?

■ Under what circumstance would the Germans *not* use Enigma?

The strategy of developing questions to explore your blind spots can strengthen project performance. It helps counteract not only herd instinct but also a range of other biases.

Status Quo Bias

The status quo bias assumes the future will be like the present, only more so. By the time of the Battle of the Bulge, the Allied High Command knew they were going to win the war. The Allies controlled the air and had a growing superiority in men and materiel. The Germans were bogged down in an unwinnable two-front war, and they could not replace their losses. Therefore, there was nothing to worry about.

That's the status quo bias in action. It's strongly reinforced by group-think.

Most of us have a strong tendency to reject the idea of discontinuity, or sudden change, even when a logical analysis suggests sudden change is easily possible. This is an example of inertia in human thinking.

But not all cognitive biases lead to wrong conclusions. Patton was at least as overconfident as any other Allied senior commander, if not more so, but he was hungry for action and motivated to look for signs the Germans were doing something innovative. He was also out of the inner circle, a function of his notorious temper, which can be a disadvantage in many ways but here insulated him from the general groupthink.

Isolation has advantages and disadvantages, so use it carefully. The best way to use it is to find people who are isolated from the inner circle by circumstances and use them as independent sounding boards. That way, you'll hear things you'll never learn otherwise.

Challenging the status quo bias must be done systematically. Instead of accepting the reflexive proposition that the burden of proof rests on the side of change, consider debating the proposal from the perspective that the burden of proof rests on the side of status quo. You may elicit far different and far more useful discussions that way.

Self-Correction

In managing blind spots, whether yours or others, the common strategy begins with awareness and then progresses into action. Challenge your own assumptions and those of your team on a regular, habitual, and systematic basis.

This is a vital strategy to follow throughout the life cycle of the project, and it is particularly important when it comes to the initiation phase, when an idea transitions across the threshold from plan to project.

3

The Most Dangerous Word
Is a Premature *Yes*

Plans are worthless, but planning is everything. There is a very great
distinction because when you are planning for an emergency
you must start with this one thing: the very definition of "emergency"
is that it is unexpected; therefore it is not going to happen
the way you are planning.
— President Dwight D. Eisenhower, speech to the National Defense
Executive Reserve Conference, Washington, D.C., 1957

The Zen of Project Initiation

The transition from discussion to taking on the role of project manager is
a delicate process, and it often sets the trajectory for project performance.
It is a critical moment, and any missteps during the transition can have
disastrous effects. Worse, the moment when a mistake is made and the
moment in which the damage from that mistake shows up can be separated by months—or even years.

We understand you may not have the option to say "no" to a new
project assignment, and even if you do have the option, we're not necessarily advising you take it. But the timing and manner of your yes is critical to achieving the desired outcome.

The PMBOK process of project initiation describes the necessary actions that take you across the threshold from idea to project. You must prepare a preliminary scope statement, identify constraints and assumptions, prepare a project charter, and get stakeholder buy-in.

Assumptions, especially those involving cognitive bias, can wreck a project before it gets started. Your first mission (whether or not you choose to accept it) is to figure out what the actual project is about. This process can be an enormously delicate and dangerous, fraught with perceptions and assumptions among stakeholders whom you may not even initially know exist.

There's a famous Zen koan: "First there is a mountain, then there is no mountain, then there is a mountain." Your first understanding of the mountain is an outline, a shape on the horizon. As you get closer, the mountain decomposes into a million individual details. Finally, you know the mountain as a whole.

When you're starting a project, there's a koan with a similar structure (see Table 3-1) but with its own particular dynamics and lessons.

Table 3-1. Zen and the Art of Project Management

Koan	Meaning
First, there is no project.	There's a problem, an opportunity—a gap.
Then there is a project.	Somebody has an idea about what should be done.
Then there is no project.	As you look at the idea more closely, all sorts of problems emerge.
Then you negotiate.	You establish a project objective and mission statement.
Then it changes.	Then it changes.

Now that you've had your moment of Zen, let's talk about war.

War for Project Managers

All wars are projects, though thankfully not all projects are wars. A war, like any other project, is temporary and unique, aimed at achieving a specific outcome. It requires planning, uses resources, can be broken down into specific work packages, has risk and uncertainty, and requires leadership.

From a project management perspective, wars include the kind with bullets and the kind without. What distinguishes a war from other types of projects is a conscious enemy, an individual or group whose purpose is to defeat your project and take some prize for their own. Perhaps that's a military enemy, or it's a race to market for a new product, or it's a duel between two vice presidents for control of the new division.

While it's a mistake to apply war thinking to all aspects of project management, there are many insights from war planning and military thinking that have direct application to the most peaceful of projects.

The Principle of the Objective

Carl Philipp Gottfried von Clausewitz joined the Prussian army as a lance corporal at the age of 12, and he worked his way up to the rank of major general. He fought in the Rhine campaigns and the Napoleonic Wars. In 1806, while serving as aide-de-camp to Prince August, Clausewitz was one of 25,000 Prussians taken prisoner when Napoleon defeated Prussia in the Battle of Jena-Auerstedt.

Returning to Prussia after two years in French captivity, he refused to accept Prussia's forced alliance to Napoleon and joined the Russian army, where he served with distinction. When Prussia freed itself from Napoleon's domination, he rejoined the Prussian army, where he served as chief of staff to the Third Prussian Corps during the battle of Waterloo.

His superiors never quite forgave him for joining the Russian army (especially because in one battle he defeated his former comrades), and so he spent more than a decade as administrative head of the General War College in Berlin, where he worked on the manuscript of his masterpiece, *On War*.

On War is most famous for the quote "War is diplomacy by other means." But that's not actually what he said. Clausewitz's insight is far more nuanced, and far more relevant to project managers: "It is of course well known that the only source of war is politics. . . . We maintain . . . that war is simply a continuation of political intercourse, with the addition of other means."

To drive home the point, Clausewitz argues that "no one starts a war—or rather, no one in his senses ought to do so—without being first clear in his mind what he intends to achieve by that war and how he intends to conduct it."

The same is true of project management. The essential question is, why? Our why involves something called "the gap"—the space between where you are and where you want to be.

The Gap

As an old sales adage puts it, no one in the world needs a power drill; what people need are *holes*. In sales, that helps you tell the difference between the *feature*, a characteristic of the product or service, and the *benefit*, the value to the customer or user. In project management, as the *PMBOK Guide* tells us, a project is a means to accomplish a desired end or to produce some desired output.

It's vital to remember that the project isn't the *end* but rather the *means*.

A project—*any* project, war or not—first exists as a gap—the gap between where you are and where you want or need to be (see Figure 3-1).

The gap is often called by other names: problem, need, opportunity, or issue. We've chosen this generic term *gap* to cover the entire range of possibilities, because if you have what you want or are already where you want to be, there's clearly no need to launch a project to get there. The gap by itself is not a project. At the outset, the project is only someone's idea of the best (or at least a possible) way to bridge the gap. Sometimes the gap is so big it can spawn multiple projects. Some gaps evolve, necessitating constant midcourse corrections.

The first step in any project is to define the gap, and the second step is to identify project options to close the gap. There may be a variety of options. For example, if the company is losing money, there is a very defi-

The Project

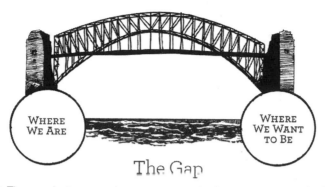

Figure 3-1. The gap between where we are and where we want to be is the essential reason for any project's existence.

nite gap between where you are and where you want to be. There may be a variety of ways to close the gap, each of which requires a very different project and often a different project manager. To improve your financial situation, you might consider any of the following:

- Reduce overhead costs

- Conduct layoffs

- Buy (or sell) a division

- Invest in a new product launch

- Change marketing, advertising, or sales strategies

Each potential strategy suggests having its own project manager, someone with different skills and experiences. The person who can slash head count isn't necessarily the same person who can run a new product launch. Project managers are seldom interchangeable. That's why top leaders spend significant time and energy finding the right project manager for the job.

The Fluid Gap

Discovering the gap is difficult enough, but the gap itself is fluid, mutating in time and space in ways difficult to predict and more difficult to manage. A big project always and necessarily has a complicated and fluid gap to be managed. To simplify the situation, identify smaller sections of the gap and think of your big project as consisting of a lot of little ones. To manage a fluid gap, you must first have an understanding of what forces cause it to flow and change. Depending on which characteristics in Table 3-2 you find in your own project, you need to add to your risk list the potential for project change that comes from those elements.

Table 3-2. The Fluid Gap

Multiplicity	The gap involves many different potential interests and benefits (along with potential liabilities and costs); any project solution must necessarily choose some interests over others and accept some costs in place of others.
Stakeholders	People want the same project for different reasons or gain the most benefit from different elements of the goal.
Circumstances	The original reason for the project becomes irrelevant or secondary based on changes in the external environment.
Analysis	The original understanding of the gap by the stakeholder or project management was incorrect, leading to a faulty project objective.
Discovery	New information, not known or knowable at the beginning of the project, comes to light.
Competition	Your actions to close the gap affect others in a negative way, and they adjust their strategies to benefit their own objectives.

Each gap implies one or more potential projects to close it. Depending on the interplay of time, cost, and necessary level of performance, and the importance of this particular gap compared to other issues, not all potential projects do (or even should) come to fruition. As a potential project manager, you need to look out for your "Old Yeller moments," when your real job is to put a bad project idea out of its misery.

Blind spots and cognitive biases can hide gaps that in retrospect appear obvious. After the fact, it's easy to see how the United States had the evidence to predict the Pearl Harbor attack, but picking salient information out of a sea of noise is much harder when you don't already know the right answer.

In addition to not seeing the gap, people can misunderstand the gap. Is the poor work performance in a particular unit a problem of mismanagement, lack of training, bad tools, weak processes, or wrong people? If the project is to fire everyone, you might succeed in the project, but you would fail to close the gap.

Here's how one manager handled a potential project with a new and demanding boss (see Figure 3-2).

Seizing the Moment

The long slog from middle management to a junior vice presidency can be uncertain and demoralizing. You hope for the moment when the

Figure 3-2. Generals Dwight D. Eisenhower (left) and George C. Marshall, Algiers Conference, June 1943.

opportunity arises for you to make your mark. Sometimes the opportunity comes years later than you expect, and the ever-present danger is that you will miss or blow your big chance.

The U.S. Army between World War I and World War II was stagnant, and many talented people languished at low ranks. One particular staff officer named Dwight David Eisenhower spent World War I training tank crews in Pennsylvania, and afterward he moved from one staff job to another, spending 16 years as a major. As a colonel, he was executive officer to General Douglas MacArthur in the Philippines.

MacArthur was a Boss from Hell, and after eight years, Eisenhower had had enough. In 1939, he demanded a transfer back to the United States, making a permanent enemy of one of the most powerful men in the Army. MacArthur, who deeply resented Eisenhower's departure and subsequent advancement, famously called him the "best clerk I ever had." (In response, Eisenhower, asked in later life by a woman whether he had met MacArthur, replied, "Not only have I met him, ma'am, I studied dramatics under him for five years in Washington and four years in the Philippines.") (Manchester, 1978)

Back in the States, Eisenhower's career reverted to type: one staff officer position after another. He made brigadier general in October 1941, quite an achievement in the peacetime army, but he had never held an active combat command. Two months into his latest assignment as executive officer of the Third U.S. Army, headquartered at Fort Sam Houston, Texas, Eisenhower received an order from Army Chief of Staff General George C. Marshall. At the time, that position was equivalent to today's chairman of the Joint Chiefs of Staff, the senior military advisor to the president.

"Come to Washington immediately," the message read.

Eisenhower could only assume the summons involved his new job assignment. His household goods had only just arrived in Texas, and his house was filled with unopened boxes. So he organized his notes on the status of the Third Army, packed his overnight bag, and arranged for military air transportation to Washington, D.C.

The trip was a disaster. His plane was forced down in a surprise December snowstorm, and Eisenhower spent two days on a train, arriving on a Sunday in a wrinkled, slept-in uniform. He headed straight for the War

Department offices on the Mall, where General Marshall was working a normal full day.

Although Eisenhower had met Marshall, he didn't know him well. This would be a fateful meeting for all concerned. The Army Chief of Staff didn't waste time on pleasantries. He launched into a 20-minute review of current and evolving U.S. war plans for the Pacific Theater. When he finished, he turned to Eisenhower and pointedly asked, "What should be our general line of action?"

This evidently caught Eisenhower completely by surprise.

Although Eisenhower had worked on the Pacific war plans in the past, he hadn't been involved in the continuous update process for months and had no idea how they might have changed. (Each plan was color coded, and there were so many different versions that they were collectively called the "Rainbow" plans.)

In addition, as a newly minted one-star general, he was hardly in a position to challenge or criticize the work of the Army's planning staff, especially not the work of Marshall, who was the Army's top general. Besides, he was ready for questions about the Third Army, not this.

He was on the spot for an answer. He had to say *something*.

Most people tend to start answering the question at this point, but that's frequently a bad idea, unless you really happen to be the World's Greatest Expert.

What Eisenhower said was, "Give me a few hours."

How Eisenhower Closed the Gap

What Eisenhower needed to figure out follows the same line of creative questioning that Clausewitz had prescribed many years earlier: first determine what needs to be done and why, and second, determine how to get it done.

What's the Project?

What's the project? As we've learned, the project is a means to close the gap. So, what's the gap? Well, that depends completely on which perspective is most useful to you at any given moment.

Programs are collections of projects the way projects are collections of tasks. But a program is not equivalent to a project the same way a project is to task, because not all programs are projects. Projects always and necessarily end; programs can be ongoing, with no planned point at which they are supposed to end. Tasks, on the other hand, share the characteristic with projects that they always have an end.

Running the Army is a program, and there's no planned point at which it's supposed to go out of business. However, the program contains any number of specific projects, along with a whole lot of operational work. A war is both a program (it contains multiple projects) and a project (temporary, unique, and full of tasks). For any project of sufficient scale or scope, there's a hierarchy of programs and projects. Let's look at that hierarchy from Eisenhower's point of view (see Table 3-3).

Table 3-3. Hierarchy of Army Programs and Projects

Level	Gap	Mission
Program (Marshall)	Armed forces are inadequate to meet current threats.	Provide a functioning army to the United States sufficient to meet its current needs.
Program (Marshall)	Military threats from Germany and Japan	Fight and win the war.
Project (MacArthur)	Military threat from Japan	Fight and win the war.
Subproject (Marshall/ MacArthur)	Weakness in U.S. Pacific forces	Provide resources to the Pacific Theater.
Subproject (Eisenhower?)	Lack of operational plans	Develop updated war plans for the Pacific Theater.
Work package (Eisenhower)	Desire for a leadership role	Impress Marshall with competence and judgment.
Task (Eisenhower)	Lack of current knowledge of Rainbow plans	Answer Marshall's question.

Few of us have been required to deal with a project decision of the magnitude that confronted Dwight David Eisenhower that cold December Sunday morning. However, many of us have been called into the boss's office and told, "I have a new project for you." There's a defining moment here, in which the first words out of your mouth can establish expectations that will shape the project for good or ill.

Although it's vital that Eisenhower have an understanding of what's involved in the entire hierarchy, his current role is limited to the subproject level and below. It's not at all sure he'll have any more than a consultative role in preparing updated war plans, so he's got two issues: his desire for a greater leadership role in the war, and his immediate need to answer Marshall's question.

It's a dangerous moment indeed. If we should be careful about saying "yes," what do we say instead?

What Do I Do Now?

Now that Eisenhower knows what has to be decided and why, how should he approach his decision? In a circumstance like this, it's important for you to identify the *minimum necessary decision and action* that must be performed *right now*. What is the smallest decision that you can make? What can you do that *isn't* irrevocable and final?

You don't necessarily have to choose the minimum necessary action. Maybe it's a good idea to go beyond the minimum. Perhaps the mission is clear, the challenge is great, and time is of the essence. But the question is still essential, "What must I decide and what must I do as a minimum *right now?*" As "right now" moves into the future, the minimum necessary decision and action changes.

The time to be most cautious is when the underlying facts and politics aren't clear and agendas are mostly hidden, if only because you're new on the scene and haven't had time to get fully oriented. If that's the case, you might want to take the attitude that "less is more."

Was there any particular reason Eisenhower needed to give a complete answer on the spot? In this case, Marshall had already waited two days for Eisenhower to arrive. And what was Marshall really asking? Did he expect Eisenhower to deliver a completely prepared briefing off the top of his head about plans he hadn't looked at for months? Our guess is probably not. From Eisenhower's point of view, there are two possibilities: Marshall believes that there is some insight that Eisenhower might have from his years of experience with General MacArthur, or Marshall is considering Eisenhower for a new role and wants to know something about him.

Either way, Eisenhower would naturally reach the same conclusion: his minimum necessary decision was to take some time to get his thoughts and ideas organized, and the associated action was to answer Marshall's direct question: "Give me a few hours."

In reality, we often go through a process like this instantaneously, reaching our conclusion without conscious thought. That's as it should be. But here in the pages of our book, we aren't in a hurry. By breaking down the detailed process when you've got time to think about it, you'll be better enabled to make the creative choice on the spot.

The big risk in "give me a few hours" is that the bar is raised. If Eisenhower's answer is good enough, the delay won't matter. If the answer is insufficient, it still won't matter; he'll have lost either way. Of course, sometimes stakes and time pressure are much greater than at other times, but it's always important to identify minimum necessary decision and action.

There's a scene in the movie *Apollo 13* (better known than the actual mission itself), in which a group of engineers has been asked to modify a carbon dioxide filter using miscellaneous junk from on board the ship so that it can be used on the lunar module. They only have an hour or so until the astronauts are incapacitated. Unlike Eisenhower's dilemma, the option of these astronauts taking a few hours to assess the job is not possible. Their minimum necessary decision is to get to work immediately, and their minimum necessary action is to complete the project before it's too late.

A Four-Hour Project

Eisenhower went to work immediately. He commandeered an empty desk and a typewriter. As he reviewed each plan, he typed out an itemized list of action steps and followed up with one-page summaries for each issue he identified, such as these:

- Supporting MacArthur's beleaguered forces in the Philippines

- Moving equipment from Hawaii

- Speeding up the slow process of mobilization

Late that afternoon, Eisenhower returned to General Marshall's office and delivered his briefing along with the typed report, laying out step by step what he proposed to do. Historian Stephen Ambrose, Eisenhower's official biographer, reports that Ike finished by saying, "We dare not fail. We must take great risks and spend any amount of money required."

Evidently, he did well enough to impress the boss.

"I agree with you," Marshall said. "Do your best to save them."

And with that, Brigadier General Eisenhower was in charge of the Philippines and Far Eastern Section of the Army War Plans Division. Two and a half years after that, he led D-Day, the greatest amphibious invasion in history.

As a rough equivalent, imagine the Scranton branch manager of a paper distributor making executive vice president in six months, and two and a half years later becoming COO/Europe for the parent conglomerate.

The Other Project Manager

What's the project? What's the gap? (See Figure 3-3.) There can be multiple and simultaneous answers, because where you stand so often depends on where you sit. No doubt Marshall really needed someone to head the War Plans group. But he had a second agenda. After giving Eisenhower his new assignment, Marshall sat back in his chair. "Eisenhower, the department is filled with able men who analyze their problems well but feel compelled always to bring them to me for final solution," he said. "I must have assistants who will solve their own problems and tell me later what they have done."

Marshall's project, you see, was recruiting project managers.

Gaps and Strategies

Identifying the gap and selecting the project strategy are arguably the most important steps in project management, so it's somewhat unfortunate that the project manager often has no direct involvement in this

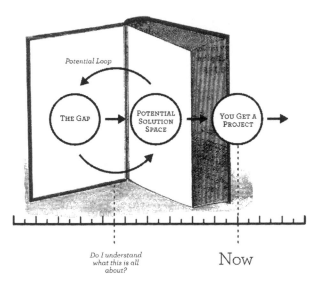

Figure 3-3. There's usually a story behind every project. If you don't know the story, you don't really understand the project.

process, certainly in the initial stages. Identification and selection are done by customers, by bosses, by users, or by others. They are the first to see the gap and the first to define it. Sometimes they do a good job of understanding the gap and selecting the solution, and you, as project manager, get a clean project scope statement.

But problems with this process are all too common. Some people fall into the "ready, fire, aim!" process of wanting immediate action. Others dither, hoping the gap will vanish as mysteriously as it appeared. Sometimes the gap is based on an assumption about the environment that will prove to be false. If you take the project handoff before you know what you've got, you may have already cemented your doom.

In our example with Marshall and Eisenhower, there are multiple gaps, and several of them are quite fluid:

■ **The hidden agenda.** The most important gap isn't necessarily the official one, or even the stated one. In this situation, it's Marshall's hidden agenda. The United States is at war, and Marshall's resources are thin indeed. He needs leaders, and he needs them quickly. When he asks for Eisenhower's opinion, he's also trying to learn something about Eisenhower the man.

■ **The official gap.** But the official gap matters too, and the quality of Eisenhower's judgment is not the only thing at issue. What's the gap between the quality of war plans as they are and the quality of war plans as we want them to be? Are the current war plans insufficient? If so, is it because there's something defective in the planning, or is it because the resources to do the job aren't there in the first place?

■ **The underlying gap.** On the eve of World War II, the American military was considered the seventeenth strongest in the world, slightly inferior to that of Romania. The overall state of the U.S. military, of course, was the fundamental gap, which would spawn an enormous array of projects. In many organizations, underlying structural issues may be the source of constant project constraints.

■ **The unknown gap.** In addition to the known gaps, there are almost certainly huge gaps that no one, from Marshall on down, even knows exist. There will be an ongoing process of discovery, and surprises are inevitable. We don't know what's in it, but we can be sure it's there.

In the initial stages of a project, especially before the work actually begins, don't assume anyone else has thought everything through yet or that the thinking has been done correctly. After all, that's one reason they need a project manager—they need someone to make a plan and to see it through. The process of analyzing everything that's happened before so you can decide what to do next is akin to working in a triage unit.

Triage for Project Managers

Your power to negotiate the circumstances and constraints of your project is greatest before you say "yes," and it deteriorates steadily over time. During your brief period of maximum power, your mission is to assess the situation and identify key options and issues. After all, you don't want to offer a premature yes to a project that turns out to be impossible. Always take a little time to assess, even if you think the project is absurdly easy or absolutely impossible. In either case, you might be wrong, and to find out, you need to conduct a triage by asking some tough questions.

Eisenhower's genius in his meeting with George C. Marshall was his ability to draw a clear, bright line around the boundaries of his project. Was it to win World War II? No, although that was clearly the overarching goal. Instead, his project was to answer the question his boss had just asked him. It took four hours from start to finish, he delivered it, and then got his prize: another bigger project.

When we imagine Eisenhower in his new role as head of the War Plans Division, we realize that his problem has changed. He no longer has a single project but rather a multiheaded Hydra that constantly spawns new projects with every one slain. New demands and new stakeholders materialize out of thin air. He's got to get limited supplies and equipment across far distances, but the supplies and equipment don't exist in the first place.

In real-world project management, we seldom encounter professionals with only a single project at a time. And even if *you* have only a single project, your organization does have others, and they all need resources. No matter how vital your mission, you're never the only game in town.

It's not enough to assess the project at hand; it's necessary to assess the portfolio of projects and ongoing work, along with the environment in which it all takes place. We must accomplish the assessment in spite of the assumptions, lack of information, and possible blind spots that we, our customers, and our stakeholders all possess.

The process for accomplishing this is known as triage.

The Hierarchy of Triage

If you've ever waited in a hospital emergency room, you know what triage is. Triage is a French word, deriving from *trier*, to sort or select. It's a formal way to prioritize medical patients based on the severity of their condition.

You don't need to do triage of any sort if you have a single patient (or project) or if there are plenty of resources to go around to accomplish all the work. But that's seldom the case. You need to perform triage from two different perspectives: not only for the project or projects for which you are responsible but also for the projects that may potentially compete for the same resources. Both relative and absolute importance have implications for what you do and how you do it. Sometimes, your job is to assert the right of way for your projects; other times the right organizational choice is to yield to others.

Your goal, remember, is to make the minimum necessary decision so you can take the minimum necessary action.

Degrees of triage range from basic to advanced, depending on what's at stake and what the issues are. Start with the basic process level, and continue as far along the journey as necessary until not only the current project but also all the projects in your environment have been accounted for.

Basic Triage

The first stage of medical triage for mass casualties is to separate the victims into three categories:

1. Those who are likely to live, regardless of what care they receive
2. Those who are likely to die, regardless of what care they receive
3. Those for whom immediate care might make a positive difference in outcome

Applying a triage perspective to project management, we can easily translate these into more familiar and useful categories: (1) projects that are likely to have a good outcome, regardless of the level of effort; (2) projects that are likely to fail, regardless of the level of effort; and (3) projects for which the level of effort might make a positive difference in outcome.

Category 1 projects can be identified by large degrees of freedom in the triple constraints of time, performance, and cost. If the schedule is very flexible, performance requirements are modest, and the budget is not at issue, there's not a lot of project management challenge. We often describe smaller Category 1 projects as "tasks," and as we've established, the difference between a task and a project is perspective. Both have the same fundamental characteristics of "temporary and unique."

Category 2 projects fall into an operational definition of impossible, which we'll explore more deeply in the Chapter 4. Placing a project in Category 2 isn't something to take lightly. Signs that a project may be in this category include being overconstrained in terms of budget or time, coming with sky-high performance requirements, and having high levels of uncontrollable risk. In such cases, you may abandon the project altogether, or perhaps you may do the very minimum exploratory activities to confirm your analysis. Of course, you may not be the only person whose opinion counts. If you think it's a Category 2 project but the boss disagrees, you may have to yield anyway.

Category 3 projects need additional analysis, but they also need action. It is in this category that most projects fall. Each determination requires an assessment of the specific current situation. What the best project managers do is make an informed situational decision using the most current information and technology to achieve the best result. (Don't forget that in a fast-changing world what is in fact impossible today may be remarkably easy a few years from now.) Let's explore this process more deeply.

Simple Triage and Rapid Treatment (START)

In responding to Marshall, Eisenhower employed a type of project triage, whether consciously or through intuition, to assess his situation and determine his next actions. Sometimes, you need to do so almost instantaneously. Other times, as in Eisenhower's case, taking time to think before committing yourself is the superior strategy. Your knowledge and experience should allow you to determine quickly whether a project is reasonable and attainable. Triage must yield to action. Some projects are simply no big deal, and the best answer is not only to avoid the premature yes but also to employ the active no. When a project seems as though it is not worth doing in the first place, it may be best not to do it at all.

Here are the two vital questions you need to ask at the very earliest stage of a potential project, as shown in Figure 3-4.

- **What am I being asked to do?** The most important initial step in receiving a project is to make sure that you understand and can confirm what it is you're actually being asked to accomplish. That doesn't mean that whatever you've been asked to do is right, or even possible; however, that's the starting point in any triage process.

■ **Is it easy and good?** At our first level of triage, our goal is to assess whether we've got a problem in the first place, because if there is no problem, you don't need an elaborate process to deal with it. "Easy" includes characteristics such as fast, simple, cheap, certain, low risk, and plenty of available resources. "Good" is whether the project is ethical, appropriate, and worth doing.

"Worth doing" can be a complicated issue. Some questions to consider are whether it provides sufficient benefits to the project manager (such as a paycheck, but also including psychic satisfaction, as with volunteer work); whether it is mutually understood by the central stakeholders; and whether or not the project process or output creates negative secondary impact (including damage to other projects or operational work). Of course, if you have too many of these questions or if they raise too many issues, the project may still be "good," but it's no longer "easy."

• **Response: do it.** If the answer to "Is it easy and good?" appears to be yes, then it's probably a good idea to just do it, but there are still questions. Will you do it now, or should you wait until later? What if your initial easy-and-good assessment is overcome by changing circumstances and new information and turns out to be wrong, à la Sewell Avery's Montgomery Ward "hold 'em" strategy? Remember, Avery's error was not in his initial assessment, which was a reasonable initial judgment, but falling victim to the cognitive biases that kept him from seeing the contrary evidence clearly.

• **Response: think about it.** If it's not clear that the answer is yes, that tells you to dig a little deeper before committing to the project. What are the issues that concern you? Are there options on how to proceed, and are there indicators as to which options may be best? How will you go about your analysis? Is there a strategic approach? Are there necessary actions? What is the next necessary step?

If the project is not easy and good, it might fall in Categories 1 or 2, projects in which the level of effort is not particularly correlated with success. If the job is not worth doing in the first place, not only is it not worth

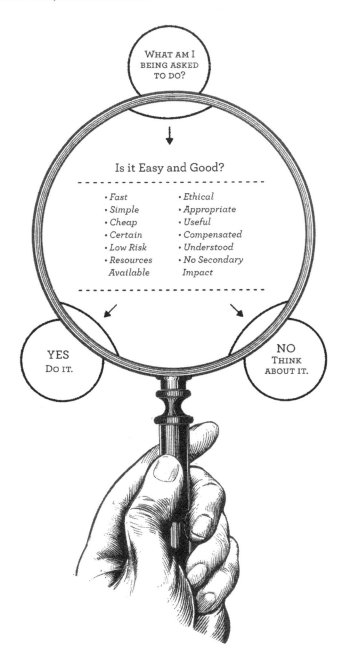

Figure 3-4. A quick and simple guide to initial project decisions.

doing well, it's better not to do it at all. Save your time and energy for activities that make a difference. If it's a Category 3 project, in which the level of effort is correlated with success, then you need to make a slightly deeper dive.

The remaining sections in this chapter focus exclusively on Category 3 projects.

PIVOT Business Triage Model

Triage systems often use a color-coding approach and a checklist process to speed classification, capture decision elements, and ensure that their interplay is understood

Business triage uses a variant on the traditional risk formula known as the PIVOT score, for its components of *probability, impact, vulnerability, outrage,* and *tolerance.* It puts the raw risk into a wider context to allow better decisions.

What follows are the definitions for all of the PIVOT elements:

- **Probability.** The likelihood of the particular event occurring (on a scale of 0 to 1, or 0 percent to 100 percent)

- **Impact.** Positive or negative impact of the event (scale: 0–3)

- **Vulnerability.** Our susceptibility to the impact (scale: 0–3)

- **Outrage.** The *expectation* of how things should be minus *satisfaction* (the perception of how things really are) (scale of each element: 0–3. If E – S is negative, use the absolute value.)

- **Threat.** The degree of enthusiasm or anger in response to the experience or event, calculated by the equation below

$$T = (P \times (I + V))^{E-S}$$

The minimum possible score is 0, the maximum is 216. This is not a linear scale. The "outrage," or difference between expectation (E) and satisfaction (S) has a disproportionate effect on the final score. It represents the likely emphasis that customers and management will place on successfully resolving the issue.

Here is a metric for conducting PIVOT triage:

1. **Green.** A project without significant threats or major issues (PIVOT score: 0–10)
2. **Yellow.** A project with some significant issues or concerns (PIVOT score: 11–64)
3. **Orange.** A project with some major issues or concerns (PIVOT score: 65–128)
4. **Red.** A project with mission-critical issues or concerns and very high levels of risk (PIVOT score: 129–216)

Project Difficulty Assessment

In our first screen of triage, we identified projects that for a variety of reasons weren't worth doing or weren't worth doing particularly well, because our efforts would not significantly affect the inevitable outcome, whether it was success or failure. In our second screen, we separated the easy-and-good projects for rapid action using the START process. In our third screen, we sorted the remaining projects using the PIVOT scale.

Our triage process has identified the most difficult and challenging projects, and now it's time to perform a deep-dive analysis of project difficulty—the final step in our preliminary analysis. The goal is to make sure we have a deeper understanding of the issues. Our earlier question, "What is the minimum decision and minimum action I must take *right now?*" is one that we must repeat as we move forward in the project. Unless you're staring at an Apollo 13–style deadline, with the clock ticking as carbon dioxide levels rise, the right thing, as innumerable after-school specials have taught us, is to Learn More About It.

The Elements of Project Difficulty

Difficulty, as noted in Chapter 1, comes in three elements: more complexity, tighter constraints, and less certainty. A project, of course, can have difficulty in more than one dimension, and their various combinations produce even more issues. (Some projects appear—and may even be—impossible. We'll show you how to manage those in Chapter 5.)

Complexity

Complexity can exist in both product and project. Project complexity is measured by such factors as the number of work packages, the number of resources, and the number of interactions and linkages. Product complexity is measured by such factors as the number of components, the number of processes, and the number of production steps. The key word here is *numbor.* Complexity can be counted.

Tools for managing complexity abound. Here are just a few:

- **Classical project management.** In building an aircraft carrier, for example, the number of work packages is measured in tens of thousands, the number of workers in thousands, and the number of subcontractors in the hundreds.

- **Systems engineering.** In designing a new computer or an automobile, millions of lines of code, thousands of electronic components, and a huge factory infrastructure have to be designed so that everything works together.

- **Logistics management.** Getting food to your grocery store or restaurant table involves the coordination of hundreds of thousands of workers, tens of thousands of vehicles, and a highly computerized, immensely complex warehousing and shipping process.

Constraints

Constraints come in many flavors, not merely the Neapolitan mélange of time, cost, and performance. You must obey applicable legislation, ethical codes, regulations, internal policies and procedures, and the laws of physics. They aren't all created equal, especially in terms of their impact on an individual project.

A constraint is only a constraint if it limits your project performance choices. If a regulation, for example, keeps you from doing something you'd otherwise do, it's a constraint. If breaking the regulation would not help you achieve your project goal, it's not a constraint but merely a fact. (We're not advocating breaking the regulation, of course, but merely classifying it in terms of your project universe.)

Constraints, as we noted, can be tight or loose, flexible or inflexible. A tight, inflexible constraint can make a project extremely difficult or even impossible. A constraint that is equally tight but has flexibility is much less serious. Equally, a loose constraint, even if inflexible, still gives you room to maneuver.

There are three fundamental strategies for managing constraints:

1. *Negotiation* to change the constraints (e.g., asking for more money, time, or resources; changing the performance requirements)
2. *Assumption analysis* to see if the constraints are actually real and necessary (e.g., that the Miami-based customer actually needs an item to work in minus 30-degree weather; that the deadline of January 4 is actually necessary to meet a summer ship date)
3. *Creativity* to see if there is an alternate way to accomplish the goal that bypasses the constraint (e.g., if it's too expensive to build a supercomputer from the ground up, perhaps a few thousand cheap computers networked together will accomplish the same thing and keep the project within budget)

Uncertainty

How firm is the ground on which your project sits? Some of the factors that govern project uncertainty include the stability and likelihood of identified assumptions, the stability of your stakeholder community, the state of competition, the extent of newness, and the level of risk. The difficulty in measuring uncertainty is the extent of the unknown unknowns universe, the extent to which we don't even know what it is we don't know. In the managing of assumptions, an equal problem comes in the form of unknown knowns, things that we don't know that we actually *do* know.

Here are some tools for managing uncertainty:

■ *Safety* is a discipline to control uncertainty by enforcing procedures and methodologies to avoid and to respond to accidents.

- *Classical risk management* uses the discipline of statistical analysis to quantify and price risks.

- *Project risk management* analyzes risks in the frequent absence of hard numerical data and develops responses to those risks.

- *Assumptions analysis* helps identify areas of uncertainty and correct for the human tendency to avoid uncertainty even when it's not beneficial.

The Levels of Project Difficulty

To make things worse, most projects tend to have more than one type of difficulty, and the whole can be sometimes greater than the sum of the parts. When complexity is complicated by tight constraints, or when uncertainty is compounded by complexity, the effects can sometimes get completely out of control.

Complex and Tightly Constrained
When complexity meets tight constraints, the value of the formal tools for managing complexity tends to increase, because driving waste out of the system and driving structural efficiency into the system reduces constraint pressure. Formal systems also provide the necessary data structure to back up negotiations to modify constraints as well as to support creative efforts to move past them.

Complex and Uncertain
Uncertainty, on the other hand, undercuts and weakens the tools needed to manage complexity. Formal systems naturally work less well when the necessary data is unavailable or unreliable. The two main tools to manage complexity and uncertainty are (1) risk management, to prepare for known possible risks, and (2) contingency reserves (e.g., extra time, extra money, and optional requirements), to prepare for unknowns.

Watch out as well for uncertainty caused by complex stakeholder interactions and political maneuvering. The trouble-plagued Denver International Airport construction project, delivered in 1994 after a $2 billion cost overrun and a year's delay, was victimized by a constant tug-of-war among stakeholders ranging from city officials to airlines to various business interests.

Cognitive biases interfere as well. Not only does weak data increase the role of bias in decision making, uncertainty can also manifest itself in the form of various biases, especially denial.

Tightly Constrained and Uncertain

Tightly constrained and highly uncertain projects are often problematic. It may be legitimate to review whether the project should even be attempted in the first place. If you go ahead with the project, failure is a significant risk, so plan for damage control in case of catastrophe. Uncertainty in a project may influence changes in the constraints as well. Negotiating changes in the constraints is usually a worthwhile strategy, but the real problem is that projects in this category are often crises responses. There were plenty of carbon dioxide filters available for the Apollo 13 lunar module; the problem was that they were on Earth. Management may freely give project teams every resource possible; the problem is that sometimes the range of what *is* possible becomes very narrow indeed.

Complex, Tightly Constrained, Highly Uncertain

The trifecta of project management comes when a project scores high in each of the three elements of difficulty. In 1991, as the Iraqi military retreated from Kuwait, they set fire to 737 oil wells after placing land mines to keep out firefighting crews. The resultant project to put out those fires fit all of our criteria. While money was available in ample amounts, professionals with the unique skills to handle such a problem are in short supply. The time constraint doesn't have a specific date attached to it, but the environmental damage was such that time pressure was enormous. Risk and uncertainty were extremely high. Commentators at the time speculated that it might not even be possible to extinguish the fires in anything less than years. The dimensions of the problem were not clear at the outset.

In a situation such as this one, you should first exploit every bit of constraint flexibility you have. If there's no give in resources or time but money is available, spend it. If you have time but no money, take more time. If there's a good-enough point within reach, aim for that. Maintain an extreme vigil over your risk portfolio. Spend resources on information. Move forward in small steps, and watch for indications that your assumptions need to be modified.

Managing Difficult Projects: Eisenhower and Operation Torch

Managing difficult projects is a problematic activity. Let's return to the story of Dwight David Eisenhower.

Eisenhower was a one-star general when he met Marshall in December 1941. By 1942, he had won his third star and an assignment as Commanding General of the European Theater of Operations. That November, he was also appointed Supreme Commander of the Allied Expeditionary Force of the North African Theater of Operations, in command of Operation Torch, the first major U.S.-led operation of World War II.

This did not go nearly as well.

A project manager's strengths in one area often serve as weaknesses in another. Knowing when we're operating out of our areas of vulnerability and bias is essential. Eisenhower, the supreme staff officer, organizer, and planner, had exceptional skills as a politician, critical for his complex role in coordinating the often-fractious Allies. But he had never held a combat command.

As a project manager, it's vital to know when you're in over your head in some areas of your project, but you don't always have the opportunity to get the help you need. Eisenhower's Operation Torch was compromised from the start.

The Soviet Union was pressuring the United States and Britain to open up a second front in Europe to take pressure off the Soviets in the east. The Americans wanted to land in Europe as soon as possible; the British believed the U.S. forces at that time would be overreaching. Instead, the allies decided to attack French North Africa, the operating area of German Field Marshal Erwin Rommel's famous Afrika Korps.

In North Africa, no one knew whether the Vichy French would fight or welcome the Anglo-American invaders. In the United States, soon-to-be-replaced military doctrine created a dual command structure for the invasion. Ground forces were under Major General George Patton, and naval forces were under Rear Admiral Henry Hewitt. Patton reported to Eisenhower, but Hewitt did not.

Logistics were problematic. Several ships arrived at the last minute. A planned coup by sympathetic French officers failed, and the French military elected to resist the landings. Casualties were high, especially when a pack of U-boats slipped in and sank four U.S. transports, several of which were still loaded, costing the Allies over 90 percent of their supplies.

Things could have been worse, but negotiations with the French resulted in a general ceasefire. Now, the inexperienced U.S. Army would face Rommel's Afrika Korps in the Battle of Kasserine Pass, which holds the record for the worst defeat inflicted on an American army by a general who was not himself an American.

What does this story say about Dwight David Eisenhower—or about us when faced with a potentially no-win project?

First, failure happens. In fact, failure is far more characteristic of senior people than of junior. When you have a great track record, you get tougher problems. The old adage says that "expenses rise twice as fast as income," and the same approximate ratio is true for problems and power.

If you can't do anything else, you can always do lessons learned, and that is also a hallmark of the truly great project manager. Dwight David Eisenhower went into the engagement without experience as a combat commander, and the campaign suffered as a result. However, the North African campaign was a crucible that transformed the inexperienced and understrength U.S. military into a formidable fighting force.

No project manager knows everything, and the wise project manager knows it. Eisenhower's "lessons learned" and post-campaign activities paved the way for the far more difficult and ultimately successful D-Day invasion of Normandy.

4

Good Enough,
Barely Adequate, Failure

Basic assumptions about reality are the paradigm of a social science,
such as management. They are usually held subconsciously by
the scholars, the writers, the teachers, the practitioners in the field.
Yet those assumptions largely determine what the discipline—scholars,
writers, teachers, practitioners—assumes to be REALITY. The discipline's
basic assumptions about reality determine what it focuses on. They
determine what a discipline considers "facts" and what it considers
the discipline itself to be about. . . . Yet, despite their importance, the
assumptions are rarely analyzed, rarely studied, rarely challenged—
indeed rarely even made explicit.
—Peter Drucker, *Management Challenges
in the 21st Century*," 1999

How Good Is "Good Enough"?

The slogan "good enough *isn't!*" is at the core of quality project management thinking, because it drives the concept of continuous improvement.
This philosophy is at the heart of W. Edwards Deming's first of the
14 points of quality: "Create constancy of purpose for the improvement of
product and service."

"Continuous improvement," however, works only for processes that don't have a planned end—or, in PMBOK speak, "operations." We can (and should) continuously improve the way we manage projects, but if we continuously improve our current project, we'll never finish. Projects, as we know, have an end point, a cost limit, and a minimum performance threshold—our old friends, the Triple Constraints.

Notice that Triple Constraints boundaries are always "worst case." A deadline is the *latest* you can get a project done; the budget is the *most* you can spend; the performance specification is the *least* you can do. In balancing the Triple Constraints, it is sometimes more valuable to exceed in certain dimensions than it is in others. Quality is not always synonymous with the performance criteria; if you're being wheeled into the emergency room, the speed may be more valuable to you than performance, as long as performance hits the minimum standard.

That's why you always have to know where "good enough" lives, whether or not you choose to aim for it in managing your project. There are often costs and trade-offs associated with exceeding good enough, and the wise project manager must understand those issues to make good choices—or, in some cases, to make the least bad choice from a host of wrong decisions.

Defining "Good Enough"

In the world of project management, it's particularly important to understand what specifically comprises good enough. Understanding what good enough means isn't the same thing as deciding to settle for it. There may be value in doing more. But more compared to what? Without a "good enough" level of project performance, you can't establish a meaningful project baseline. Worse, the common quality standard "exceeding customer expectations" becomes meaningless. How exactly are you supposed to exceed expectations unless they've been established in the first place?

But should you always necessarily try to exceed expectations? That's the assumption behind "good enough *isn't*." Of course, in a literal sense, the phrase seems self-contradictory: how can "good enough" possibly not be good enough? A closer look at "good enough" reveals the answer: the phrase means two different things. Sometimes, good enough is a synonym for "fully satisfactory." That kind of good enough is really good enough. And sometimes good enough (usually said with a grimace or a dismissive hand gesture) means "barely adequate."

In all, we've identified seven levels that cover the full range of project outcomes. They are, from best to worst:

1. Perfect
2. Outstanding
3. Exceeds expectations
4. Fully satisfactory
5. Barely adequate
6. Failure
7. Catastrophe

Together, they form the basis for a tool we call the Seven Level Outcome Evaluation, a powerful process that provides you with the questions and insights necessary to point your project toward the right outcome.

Seven Level Outcome Evaluation

When you perform a Seven Level Outcome Evaluation of your project, you combine quality and risk assessment and link both to the project and its environment. This is in line with modern quality concepts, all of which require that quality be defined in some measurable way rather than be presented as an indefinable quality of "goodness." As President Bill Clinton once said: "It ain't dog food if the dog don't eat it." Faux quality benefits no one; it's gold plating. Real quality provides measurable benefits to a group of stakeholders.

In project management, quality and risk are inextricably tied together. To make informed and effective decisions about quality, one must understand the complete operational context. Table 4-1 defines the seven levels of performance outcome in more detail.

Table 4-1. The Seven Levels of Project Outcomes

Outcome	Definition
Perfect	A perfect project outcome sometimes exists only in theory. It involves no compromises or trade-offs and fulfills all customer expectations, hopes, and dreams.
Outstanding	An outstanding project outcome is as close to perfect as can be reasonably expected in a constrained world. Deliverables far exceed expectations, and everybody's reputation benefits.
Exceeds expectations	A project that exceeds expectations delivers more than the basics, better than the basics, and often either faster or cheaper than the basics.
Fully satisfactory	A fully satisfactory project meets the traditional rubric of on time, on budget, and to spec.
Barely adequate	A barely adequate project delivers the lowest level of performance we can get away with not calling actual failure.
Failure	A failed project does not achieve the minimum acceptable outcome in one or more key elements.
Catastrophe	A catastrophe creates more collateral damage than the success of the project would have created good.

Operational Definition of Outcomes Exercise

To implement this hierarchy for a specific project, first write an operational definition of outcomes for each level. There are three immediate benefits from performing this exercise. First, by identifying the higher levels of performance, we must assess the risk/cost/reward ratios, identify the different possible areas of success, and establish a target level of performance. Second, by identifying the lower levels of performance, we identify key risks and ensure we have project response strategies and resources to deal with them. Finally, by identifying the fully satisfactory level of good enough, we establish the central performance benchmark against which we measure each level of the hierarchy.

Perfect

To determine what would be perfect, broaden your perspective regarding the real underlying values that should drive your project. To take the project of publishing this book as an example, there are obvious elements to what would be considered perfection: most of us would choose, if possible, to produce an enduring business classic that dominates the bestseller list for the next several decades. Drilling down, however, we can discover there are more specific goals.

The process of establishing goals often involves some detective work. While some goals are obvious and clear from the outside, others are hidden from view, at least initially. Only when we start questioning our environment, brainstorming creative options, and analyzing potential strategies are we able to discover in detail how the goal works.

Some hidden goals, like some hidden agendas, involve deliberate concealment on somebody's part, but most hidden goals are covered up by blind spots, cognitive biases, and assumptions. We need to probe in order to find them. If our project is to write a book, what's the gap? What are we trying to bridge? Is writing a book the best strategy to close the gap? Is it sufficient? Are there other considerations? What should the book accomplish for us? There are a range of answers, and some of them are not necessarily clear before the project gets under way.

Projects can provide both direct benefits (book = royalty) and indirect benefits (book = speaking engagements). They may provide psychological benefits (book = ego gratification), serve as attack or defense (book = reputation), or solve problems (book = tenure).

A single project can offer multiple benefits. Some benefits are mutually reinforcing (high sales = bigger royalties = more speaking engagements). Others may work against each other (ego gratification ≠ better sales). There's a hierarchy of benefits, and which hierarchy you choose has implications for the style, content, and market for the book. If a project has multiple stakeholders, the problem adds a new order of complexity. Each stakeholder may have a different set of potential benefits and a different hierarchy of values.

It's easy to optimize a project for a single benefit. More often, the creative project manager has to figure out how to optimize the mix. As noted project management author J. Davidson Frame famously observed, "Optimization of the whole often requires suboptimization of the parts."

But your purpose is to define *perfect*. To define *perfect*, you need to first list all the potential benefits, not only to you but also to all the other stakeholders. What is the ideal outcome for each individual benefit? By understanding *perfect* you can often find additional benefits or ways to achieve higher levels of existing benefits so there's more value to go around. Quality doesn't always cost more. Pick the "low-hanging fruit."

Outstanding

Now let's take it down a notch. Looking at perfection helps us grow the pie and understand the stakeholders. But there's more to learn. What's the highest level of performance we could practically achieve short of perfection, and what would it take to achieve it? In producing a book, writing it is only one element. As any publisher or editor will tell you, the authors' willingness to publicize the book may have a far greater influence on the book's eventual success. By studying *outstanding*, the creative project manager's goal is to find secondary elements of the project that provide value in closing the gap.

Pay close attention to things that appear on first glance to be impossible. First, if you become aware that something is impossible, that is so usually because there would be some value in it if it could be done. Perhaps there's an alternate strategy. Perhaps you've found a key risk. Perhaps a partial solution would provide a disproportionate amount of value.

Exceeds Expectations

Publishers, like any other businesspeople, invest where they have an expectation of return. What level of performance would persuade the publisher to make a greater investment in our future books? What would make them want to keep us happy in return?

At the exceeds expectations level, you focus on detailed customer needs, especially in the small stuff. There's almost always something that may not bear directly on the gap but that makes the lives of your immediate customers go more smoothly. The first-line customers may be several steps away from the ultimate end users, but they often have disproportionate influence in whether you get your next job.

Fully Satisfactory

Fully satisfactory performance doesn't get awards or extravagant praise. It's the expected level of performance, and it's usually expressed in Triple Constraints terms: on time, on budget, and on spec. This is the good enough that's good enough. In our case, the deadline is fixed by contract. Our editor gets to decide whether we met performance, but there are some general standards that allow us to have some degree of confidence when we turn in a manuscript. Budget (at least the writing budget) is our problem, not the publisher's. We get an advance against royalties, but our expenses and the value of our time come out of that.

Barely Adequate

There's a range between the level of professionalism an editor expects and the level of professionalism an editor will accept. Authors are often late, manuscripts are improperly formatted, word counts are ignored, and follow-through is weak. Depending on a book's sales, an author's professional stature, and other factors, these shortcomings may not be enough for a publisher to drop an author, but they certainly don't help.

There are circumstances in which barely adequate is quite excusable. Sometimes situations are beyond anyone's control, and in such cases, getting something done even at a minimum level may be considered a remarkable achievement.

Failure

Any level of performance that results in the publisher not wanting to work with us again would be a failure. That encompasses failures in the writing process and also in the marketing process. The purpose of looking at the conditions of failure is to decide on the key risks of the project. We've written enough that we're reasonably confident of delivering an acceptable manuscript; risk of failure is low.

Is failure to deliver an acceptable manuscript the only kind of failure? Well, no. There are a lot of reasons why a book may not be enough of a success to win future opportunities, some controllable, some less so. We'll get into risk management in a later chapter, but for now, a first draft of a list of major opportunities to fail is a good part of your thinking process.

Catastrophe

What's the worst that could possibly happen? We could make a huge, embarrassing blunder that ruins our reputation. We could commit libel or plagiarism and face legal repercussions. This is why authors double-check their facts and cite sources, and it's one of the reasons editors review manuscripts.

Even when catastrophe is unlikely, we need to know what it is and where it lives. Many basic procedures (e.g., fact checking of a manuscript) that we take for granted exist to make sure catastrophes don't happen. The danger is that sometimes we find ourselves lulled into a false sense of security and don't give these procedures the attention they deserve.

Now let's apply this concept on a more substantial specific project: the infamous Ford Pinto, best remembered today for its defective gas tank.

Seven Level Outcome Evaluation — the Ford Pinto

First, some background: In 1968, Ford Motor Company executives decided to add a subcompact automobile to their product line, responding to a minor but increasingly troublesome threat from carmakers overseas, such as Volkswagen, Datsun, and Toyota. Other U.S. automakers were also eyeing the same market segment. The Gremlin, from American Motors Corp. (AMC), was the first to market, followed by the Chevrolet Vega. The Ford Pinto was the third to market — introduced one day after the Vega. An entry-level Pinto sold for $1,850 (a little over $11,000 in 2008 dollars).

So, we have an idea of the gap: position a new vehicle to be competitive in a new market segment threatened by (currently minor) competition overseas. The design specs were established by then Ford president Lee Iacocca: a small car that wasn't to weigh an ounce over 2,000 pounds and not cost a cent over $2,000. It was important for the car to reach the market quickly. As a result, the Pinto schedule was established at just under 25 months, a challenging target, because the normal time span from conception to production at Ford at the time was about 43 months.

Now, on to the evaluation. The value of performing a Seven Level Outcome Evaluation is that it gives you a picture of your objectives in both quality and risk. By defining the higher levels of outcome, you identify operational elements of quality; by defining the lower levels, you identify key risks.

Given the competitive environment and corporate circumstances at the time, a Seven Level Outcome Evaluation of the proposed Ford Pinto might have looked like Table 4-2.

Table 4-2. Seven Level Outcome Evaluation of the Ford Pinto

Outcome	Definition
Perfect	The Ford Pinto is the outstanding leader in subcompact cars. Its quality reputation far exceeds that of its competitors, foreign and domestic. Its cost is significantly below competition, and its profitability is high. The styling is a hit with its target demographic. Foreign and domestic competition is left in the dust.
Outstanding	The Ford Pinto dramatically exceeds sales expectations and is a runaway hit. Quality, cost, and styling are above competitive benchmarks. Ford steadily increases market share for target demographic.
Exceeds expectations	The Ford Pinto is competitive with the best of its class, and sales figures reflect its superior yet slow market penetration. The car is profitable to make and sell.
Fully satisfactory	A true subcompact in size and weight. Low cost of ownership, including initial price, fuel consumption, reliability, and serviceability. Clear product superiority in appearance, comfort, features, ride and handling, and performance. (from the product objectives in the Pinto *Green Book*, a top-secret Ford manual)
Barely adequate	The Pinto is a profitable addition to the Ford line, but it lags behind competitors. Ford will have to improve the car substantially in subsequent model years if it hopes to achieve higher levels of performance and market share.
Failure	The Pinto fails to meet acceptable sales or profitability targets. The market reception ranges from tepid to poor; competitive cars dominate the market, and Ford is an also-ran in the subcompact class. The investment continues to lose money, draining corporate resources.
Catastrophe	The Ford Pinto seriously damages Ford's reputation and financial position by having significant safety or reliability problems.

Now that we've defined the seven levels, what next? Well, to define "good enough," we need to interpret this information by establishing two benchmarks in the seven levels. Doing so gives us a new gap, the one between what we *can* do under normal conditions and what we *need* or *want* to do, and that's another measure of the difficulty of the project. If what we need to do is *less* than what we can do normally, the project is easy. If what we need to do is *more* than we can do normally, then it is hard. One step above that, there is a danger it may be impossible.

That's why it's vital to establish the following two benchmarks:

1. The lowest level of performance achievable *without extraordinary effort*
2. The desired level of performance that will close the gap that led to the project in the first place

From our perspective at the beginning of the Pinto project, here's how to set these benchmarks.

Our first benchmark is to define the lowest level of performance achievable without extraordinary effort. Ford hasn't produced a car for this price point since 1958. Keeping costs low, within the company's current cost structure, places significant constraints on the project. It will require significant effort for the Pinto project team to achieve a level of barely adequate.

The second benchmark is the level of performance that will close the gap that led to the project in the first place. In addition to the official *Green Book* performance criteria, it's clear that the real (if not articulated) purpose of the Pinto project is to close the gap in the Ford product line, make Ford a successful player in the subcompact market, and at least meet the threat low-cost imports pose to the company. That's the exceeds-expectations level.

Here are the benchmarks for the Seven Level Outcome Evaluation as applied to the Ford Pinto project:

1. The lowest level of performance achievable without extraordinary effort is *barely adequate.*

2. The desired level of performance that will close the gap that led to the project in the first place is *exceeds expectations*.

In this instance, the project manager has only limited control over all the elements. Executive management sets design criteria; the competition establishes competitive benchmarks; customers define customer satisfaction. Understanding both the context as well as the specifics is essential for the project manager because it illuminates the difficult situation the project manager must navigate. For example, authority over corporate resources may be outside the charter of the project manager. Achieving "exceeds expectations" has a lot to do with marketing, not just with design, yet those resources may not be under the control of the project manager. And of course, what the competition does is never under the control of the project manager.

So now, our picture of the gap has evolved. It's more nuanced, and we're discovering more of the issues, both threat and opportunity.

Given the gap between the level of easy performance and desired performance, what can we do? Here's a partial list of potential strategies for managing the Pinto project:

1. Spend extraordinary amounts of noncompensated overtime to get the job done right, by brute force if necessary
2. Modify the time and cost constraints to give engineers and designers the resources to create a remarkable design, offering the car as a temporary loss leader to conquer a new market
3. Achieve a creative breakthrough that renders current time and cost constraints obsolete, and build a remarkable new car on time and on budget
4. Realize a level of performance somewhere between barely adequate and fully satisfactory in the first model year, and incrementally improve the product over time so that it eventually achieves established performance goals

Option 1 requires hard work and risks staff burnout; Option 2 requires successful negotiation; Option 3 requires successful creativity;

Option 4 is the default. It seems this project will do well if it delivers something above barely adequate, even if it's not all the way to fully satisfactory in the first model year, as long as there's a strategy for improvement.

The Godzilla Principle: Managing the Potential Catastrophe

In Japanese monster movies, there's often a scene in which the monster du jour, whether Mothra or Ghidra or Godzilla himself, appears as a baby. Only one prescient scientist (or young kid) recognizes the threat or opportunity; everyone else ignores it until the creature is destroying downtown Tokyo.

In project management, it's pretty much the same story.

Too often, the potential catastrophe is overlooked, perhaps because it's unlikely, and sometimes (ironically) because it's too obvious. Yet catastrophe often lurks even in the simplest of projects. We can't afford to rely on the equivalent of a prescient scientist or young kid from the monster movie (and we know from bitter experience that no one ever listens to that person anyway, at least not until it's too late).

A key strategy for the creative project manager is to look for the potential for catastrophe in any project. No matter how subtle, no matter how improbable, you can't afford to ignore that baby monster. If you can't see the potential catastrophe, it's hidden by a cognitive bias. One reason it might be hard to find is that you already have procedures in place to deal with it. Ask yourself, "What routine procedures do I follow, and why do I follow them?"

For example, notice that in the Pinto Seven Level Evaluation, safety and engineering only appear in the definition of catastrophe, and not at any higher outcome. The potential impact of safety and engineering are only measured in the negative — catastrophic defects.

It's vital to note that the reciprocal is not automatically true.

Superior safety doesn't show up in any of the higher definitions. There was, in fact, no mention of safety in the key project objectives because Ford *assumed* safety. Its competent engineers would surely avoid any serious mistakes, no matter how starved for resources.

Notice the cognitive blind spot settling gently over the landscape.

Before production began, Ford engineers identified a flaw in the gas tank design. In a rear-end impact exceeding 25 miles per hour (mph), the Pinto's rear would crumple right up to the back seat. This ripped off the tube leading to the gas tank cap, causing gasoline to spill. The gas tank would buckle as well, jamming up against the differential housing, where four protruding bolts could easily tear additional holes in the tank. A single spark could trigger catastrophe. At impacts over 40 mph, doors would often jam, meaning that passengers could not escape the flames.

Was this flaw presented to management, especially to project manager Lee Iacocca? One engineer who worked on the Pinto said, "Whenever a problem was raised that meant a delay on the Pinto, Lee would chomp on his cigar, look out the window and say, 'Read the product objectives and get back to work.'"

In an infamous risk analysis prepared for the National Highway Traffic Safety Administration (NHTSA), Ford concluded that the cost/benefit equation mandated against a recall. Figure 4-1 shows the relevant detail.

Benefits and Costs Relating to Fuel Leakage Associated with the Static Rollover Test of the Ford Pinto

BENEFITS:
Savings—180 burn deaths, 180 serious burn injuries, 2,100 burned vehicles
Unit Cost—$200,000 per death, $67,000 per injury, $700 per vehicle
Total Benefits—180 × ($200,000) + 180 × ($67,000) + 2,100 × ($700) =
        $49.5 million.

COSTS:
Sales—11 million cars, 1.5 million light trucks
Unit Cost—$11 per car; $11 per truck
Total Cost—11,000,000 × ($11) + 1,500,000 × ($11) = $137 million

---

Figure 4-1. This information is taken from an interoffice report from Ford's Environmental and Safety Engineering Department, "Fatalities Associated with Crash Induced Fuel Leakage and Fires," by E. S. Grush and C. S. Saunby. It was prepared in response to a NHTSA request, and the cost figures involving human lives were drawn from standard NHTSA numbers. Although this report has been used as evidence of Ford callousness, this report discusses all subcompacts, not merely the Pinto. ($49.5 million 1968 = $302 million 2009; $137 million 1968 = $836 million 2009).

There's some doubt whether the document shown in Figure 4-2 was used for internal decision making about the Ford Pinto or was simply a routine filing with the NHTSA that had nothing directly to do with the Pinto gas tank decision. Either way, when the document leaked in 1977, it was as incendiary as the gas tanks themselves.

According to the memo, it would have cost $11 per unit ($67 in 2009 dollars) to fix the problem. Other reports point out that Ford could have inserted a rubber bladder in the gas tank that would have prevented spillage for only $5.08 per unit ($31 in 2009 dollars), although the cost/benefit equation would still tip in favor of paying accident victims ($63.5 million to fix the problem versus $49.5 million to pay for it, or $388 million versus $302 million in 2009 dollars). The story of the Pinto is, not surprisingly, held up as a textbook case for companies putting profit ahead of people. However, the problem is a bit more complicated than that.

How could Ford executives behave that way? Unfortunately, cognitive bias was at work—two cognitive biases in particular.

The Semmelweis Reflex

Besides the threat from low-cost German and Japanese imports, there were other environmental factors that affected the project. A Washington, D.C.–based consumer advocate named Ralph Nader had recently published the bestselling *Unsafe at Any Speed*, exposing safety shortfalls in American automobiles. The fallout was significant. After highly public congressional hearings, the Consumer Protection Agency was established and a stream of safety regulations and associated litigation followed, which to some extent continues to this day.

As we've seen in Chapter 1, the Semmelweis reflex kicks in whenever one person accuses other people of moral turpitude. The result is denial and resistance, which is the exact opposite of the desired effect. Unfortunately, it's human nature to resist the accusation of immoral behavior, especially when you had no ill intent. As noted, Ford executives weren't callously ignoring safety; they were assuming it.

The Normalcy Bias

People tend to underestimate both the likelihood of catastrophe and its impact, which is a danger for anyone preparing a risk management plan.

It's also one reason why so many people don't construct a risk management plan in the first place.

The first consequence of the normalcy bias is failing to prepare adequately for catastrophe. If warning signs appear on the horizon, the normalcy bias leads us to interpret the signs in the most hopeful way possible, exploiting anything ambiguous in the data to confirm that, yes, all is well.

Root Causes of Catastrophe

Pay particular attention to the definition and root cause of catastrophe. Here are some questions to consider:

- **Is it a risk you're already subconsciously aware of and that you already work toward mitigating?** Authors fact-check their books; engineers test their designs; auditors verify accounting data; doctors wash their hands. These everyday procedures exist because of the ever-present possibility of disaster. We enter a danger zone when processes become routine and perceptions get blurred. Do your processes need improvement or rejuvenation?

- **Is it a risk you weren't aware of but can easily mitigate?** Almost any bottle you buy today comes with a tamper-evident seal, but that type of packaging began only after the 1982 Chicago Tylenol murders, which we will discuss later in this chapter. We establish new processes and methods as our risk awareness grows. Are there new risks or issues we need to deal with?

- **Is it a risk that can't be reduced to an acceptable threshold?** Living in a constant high-risk environment elevates risk management processes to a central position in everything you do, such as the extra cost of complying with earthquake codes in San Francisco. Which risks do we have to live with?

- **Is it a risk in a minor area of your project?** Design standards necessarily emphasize some goals over others. If catastrophe lurks in an element of the project that would otherwise rightly receive short shrift, then it needs to be elevated in importance. Does catastrophe lurk in an unusual corner?

■ **Does this risk require you to make trade-offs between virtues you independently uphold?** Customers value safety, but they also value price, styling, and many other elements of a car. Each element often has a minimum standard of acceptance, but anything above that is subject to discussion. Is there a conflict among virtues on this project?

■ **Is there a cognitive or decision-making bias preventing this risk from being correctly seen?** Biases often obscure important issues; that's why they're dangerous. When the environment is delicate, you must carefully assess the biases in yourself and others in order to figure out what you can and should do about them. What are we not seeing? What has changed?

Deciding What's Good Enough

It's difficult to discuss the Ford Pinto situation without sidetracking into the field of business ethics; "good enough" encompasses morality and ethics as well as operational requirements. It's dangerous to omit ethical considerations in formulating a project management strategy.

Ethical decisions intertwine with business decisions; that's why there's a field called business ethics. In our particular line of work, we are fortunate that there's often no business contradiction between doing the right thing and doing the smart thing. Good corporate character is certainly a business asset, and we're all familiar with the dangers of stepping on the slippery slope.

When Virtues Are Incompatible

Unfortunately, sometimes virtues are not compatible. We rightly value honesty, and we rightly value kindness. Unfortunately, there are situations in which we can't practice both. We have to calibrate the damage to each virtue and make a values-based decision according to the specific circumstances. We are forced onto that slippery slope, like it or not, and the saddest of all words are often these: "It seemed like a good idea at the time."

The toughest job in decision making is choosing between bad and worse, a choice between violating one standard of desirable behavior and violating another. No company likes laying off employees, but no company likes or can tolerate losing money for long periods of time. These decisions tend to float up the organizational ladder. The higher you are, the worse the choices that land on your plate. Human nature is to deny the dilemma; we often blind ourselves to one part of the problem in order to convince ourselves of the rightness of our own choices.

In the case of the Ford Pinto, pricing the Pinto too high would have been a bad decision. It would have risked making the car economically uncompetitive, which certainly would have qualified it as a project failure. But incorporating a potentially exploding gas tank would have negative consequences as well. If Ford couldn't find a way to keep the price low *and* the gas tank from exploding, it had three potential choices: cancel the project, keep the price low, or fix the gas tank problem.

Just because all your choices have problems doesn't excuse you from the necessity of making a choice.

How Do Decisions Get Made?

How could people make a decision like this? Our purpose here is neither to condemn nor excuse Ford's decision but rather to understand it. With the benefit of hindsight it's easy to see that Ford was wrong, but that's a benefit the decision makers did not have at the time. When virtues and values collide, it's difficult sometimes to see the full ramifications of decisions. That's why we say, "It seemed like a good idea at the time." The decision never looks as clear-cut at the present time as it does later.

Cars provide enormous benefits, and they also kill people. In 2008, 43,313 people died in U.S. automobile accidents. That's a terrible number, but we all accept that we take our lives—and those of our passengers—in our hands every time we get behind the wheel. If you're in the auto industry, you have to accept that fact. Cars can be safer, but it's probably not possible to engineer out all the risk, and it's certainly not possible to do so without making unacceptable compromises in other areas.

What's an acceptable number? In practice, we establish benchmarks. Toyotas and Volkswagens and AMC Gremlins also have accidents. What is the average for this class of car? Is the Ford Pinto better or worse than its competition? As measured by occupant fatalities per million cars in operation during 1975 and 1976, Pinto numbers were in fact comparable to those of its competitors'. At least internally, that qualifies as an acceptable level of risk.

How it will sound in a newspaper exposé or in a courtroom may be a very different story.

Making Business Sense of Ethical Choices

You need not fully agree with this analysis, but it's important for us to see it from Ford's point of view. When we are asked to make safety/performance trade-offs, or trade-offs in any area, we normally benchmark according to the standards of our industry. But let's go back to the analysis. Our Seven Level Outcome Evaluation is very clear: if a safety or reliability problem causes damage to Ford's reputation or finances, it's a catastrophe. This point alone should have ensured that Ford leadership took the gas tank issue seriously, although the Semmelweis reflex stood squarely in the way.

The answer is not as simple as "put safety at the top of the list." In human motivation, we distinguish between *motivators* that change behaviors and *satisfiers* that only cause problems when they aren't present. Being treated with respect is a motivator; getting a paycheck every two weeks is a satisfier. For Ford customers, safety wasn't a motivator, it was a satisfier. The problem with safety comes only when it *isn't* there. Watch out for the assumption that the upside and the downside are always reciprocal; sometimes the upside is as simple as the avoidance of a downside.

What Most Cost/Benefit Analyses Don't Address

A proper cost/benefit analysis needs to consider a range of assumptions. For example, Ford used the $200,000-per-death figure from NHTSA, but other federal standards ranged as high as $350,000 per death. According to the first measure, the total cost of the deaths is $49.5 million. Change to the higher number, and it goes to $76 million. When you do the analysis based on a single standard, you get a single number, but it may be far smarter to calculate the range.

To make sure your cost/benefit analysis is really useful, you must ask yourself whether you've actually found all the potential costs.

For example, the real cost to Ford will be what is awarded by the courts. That, of course, will be influenced by how a jury will react if they should discover that the cost of fixing the problem was $11 per unit. Ford's risk analysis ignored the likelihood of this information slipping out. Considering the range of people at Ford who knew about it, the number of lawyers conducting discovery, and general press interest in the subject, the chance of this kind of information being exposed seems fairly high.

Even using conservative assumptions that there was no more than a 50 percent chance of the information getting out, and that only 25 percent of the cases will result in significant damage awards, the cost to Ford for deaths alone would approach $180 million, significantly more than the $137 million needed to fix the problem with the gas tank. And that number, in turn, neglects the economic impact of damage to Ford's reputation and brand identity.

Finally, after everything else, Ford was forced to do a Pinto recall and fix the gas tanks anyway. It would have been far, far cheaper for Ford to fix the problem in the first place; as we have seen, the data existed for Ford to make a better decision. That's why it's vital to define, understand, and plan to mitigate catastrophe.

Whenever the press of events and objectives focuses your attention on a single area, it becomes vital to look at the problem through different frames. With the Ford Pinto, emphasis was on how to achieve the higher outcome levels rather than how to avoid catastrophe, with the result that the baby monster had plenty of opportunity to grow to full Godzilla size and ravage Detroit.

When attention becomes centered on catastrophe, on the other hand, it may be a good opportunity to focus on perfection, if for no other reason than to provide a different frame through which to view the situation.

What's the upside of your downside?

Seven Level Outcome Evaluation — Tylenol Damage Control

We've recommended using the Seven Level Outcome Evaluation to deepen your understanding of any given project. Let's see what it might reveal in the famous case of the poisoned Tylenol.

Extra Strength Murder

On the morning of September 29, 1982, Mary Kellerman, a 12-year-old girl living in the Chicago suburb of Elk Grove Village, took a capsule of Extra Strength Tylenol and died almost immediately. Six other victims died in short order. As soon as investigators discovered the common link, the warning system went into overdrive. Police went so far as to broadcast warnings over loudspeakers as patrol cars fanned out through neighborhoods.

A total of eight poisoned bottles were eventually found. Five of them had already done their dirty work; three more were found on shelves. Sabotage during the production process was ruled out (the bottles came from different factories), and police theorized that the murderer had bought or stolen the Tylenol, replaced some of the pills with cyanide, and put the packages back on retail shelves in supermarkets and drugstores.

Imagine you're the president of Johnson & Johnson, the parent company of McNeil Consumer Healthcare, makers of Tylenol. What do you do? (See Table 4-3.)

Table 4-3. Seven Level Outcome Evaluation of the Response to the Tylenol Murders

Outcome	Definition
Perfect	The company's response to the incident is universally praised as courageous, decent, and humane. Any dip in sales or stock price is short lived, and the reputation and identity of Johnson & Johnson, McNeil, and the Tylenol brand are actually enhanced as a result of the company's behavior during this tragedy. Sales surge past previous levels.

Outstanding	The company's response to the incident is generally recognized as excellent. Any dip in sales or stock price is short lived, and the reputation and identity of Johnson & Johnson, McNeil, and the Tylenol brand are maintained as a result of the company's behavior during this tragedy. Tylenol sales quickly rebound to normal.
Exceeds expectations	The case is resolved quickly and conclusively, and the company is declared innocent of liability. There are some short-term costs and a dip in sales, but the reputation and identity of Johnson & Johnson, McNeil, and the Tylenol brand are not permanently affected. Tylenol returns to pre-incident sales levels within six months to a year.
Fully satisfactory	There are significant short-term costs, and the company's sales and stock price suffer in the short run. The reputation and identity of Johnson & Johnson, McNeil, and the Tylenol brand recover quickly. With significant marketing efforts, Tylenol returns to pre-incident sales levels within a year to 18 months.
Barely adequate	There are major short-term costs, and the company's sales and stock price suffer in the short and medium term. The reputation and identity of Johnson & Johnson, McNeil, and the Tylenol brand are not damaged substantially. Even with significant marketing efforts, Tylenol takes two to five years to return to pre-incident sales levels.
Failure	The Tylenol line becomes so tainted that it has to be retired. Costs to the company are substantial, leading to significant drop in market value and reputation.
Catastrophe	The incident becomes a major scandal, and the company is implicated, whether fairly or unfairly. Legal costs are substantial; sales and stock price plummets as the contagion spreads across brand lines. The company is at risk of being broken up, sold, or reorganized.

Setting Benchmarks

Remember, the two benchmarks you need to identify are (1) the highest level of accomplishment you can achieve *without extraordinary effort,* and (2) the desired performance level that will close the gap that led to the project in the first place.

The First Benchmark

As advertising guru Jerry Della Femina said to the *New York Times,* "I don't think they can ever sell another product under [the Tylenol] name. There may be an advertising person who thinks he can solve this, and if they find him, I want to hire him, because then I want him to turn our water cooler into a wine cooler." The implication is that the highest level you can achieve without extraordinary effort is *failure.*

The real situation may be a little better than that. The incident appears to have nothing to do with McNeil's manufacturing or quality control processes. It's obvious the murderer could have chosen any packaged product to adulterate with cyanide; the poisoning is not a flaw in the product. Unless further investigation should reveal an unexpected culpability on the part of Johnson & Johnson or McNeil, or a false rumor about the product takes hold in the public imagination, catastrophe is unlikely.

That would give us a first benchmark of *barely adequate.*

The Second Benchmark

The company expects consequences, and it's unlikely they expect the project team to do more than contain the damage. An outcome of *fully satisfactory* would probably exceed the realistic expectations of the company; a level of *barely adequate* would probably be acceptable, given the level of challenge.

The two benchmarks are identical. The company can achieve barely adequate without extraordinary effort, and a result of barely adequate would address the gap in a satisfactory manner. That's clearly good news.

However, as we've discussed, knowing where good enough lives (in this case, at the barely adequate level) doesn't automatically imply that good enough should be the target at which to aim. There's substantial value to the company if it's able to do better than the minimum, so it's probably worth the time to look at the higher levels of potential outcome.

In doing so, project managers don't want to commit the error of "making perfect the enemy of good (enough)." But creative project managers always make sure they consider multiple options before they settle on a final choice.

Here's our next essential project management question, "What could we achieve if we really put our minds to it, and would it be worth it?"

Avoiding Catastrophe/Achieving Perfection

As we've learned in our Ford Pinto analysis, it's always vital to take a hard look at the catastrophe scenario. The initial evidence suggests that there is no company fault in this situation. It's still probably a good idea to conduct an internal review of quality assurance processes both related to the specific incident and in general. It's also a good idea to put public relations resources on high alert to combat false rumors. If there's a catastrophe brewing, you want to deal with the baby Godzilla rather than attempt to smite the full-grown variety.

The creative project manager should always also ask the counterintuitive question. In the Tylenol case, the mental focus trends naturally toward catastrophe, which indicates that it's a good idea to reframe the point of view to look at the opposite end. Could a disaster of this magnitude be turned into something that actually *advances* the company's reputation?

The Johnson & Johnson Response

The Johnson & Johnson public relations project undertaken in response to the 1982 Tylenol poisonings has reached the status of legend. The strategy had two phases: (1) responding to the immediate crisis, and (2) rebuilding the brand reputation. The first phase, of course, was the mandatory underpinning of the second. Had the company not behaved extraordinarily well, the strategy to reestablish the Tylenol brand likely would have failed.

Responding to the immediate crisis, the company issued a nationwide recall of all Tylenol products—not just the capsules implicated in the actual murders—removing 31 million bottles worth over $100 million at retail. To further rebuild the brand reputation, it switched advertising strategies to increase warnings to consumers. Once it was determined that only capsules had been adulterated, Johnson & Johnson offered to exchange all Tylenol capsules for solid tablets, regardless of date of purchase.

The Value of Early Study

The IBM System Science Institute (2002) reported that the cost of fixing a problem in the maintenance stage of a product's life cycle was 100 times more expensive than fixing the same in the design stage. The cost savings can be even more dramatic when you catch the problems (or better yet, find the opportunities) when you're still in the conceptual stages.

People tend to think of creative thinking as the opposite of structured thinking, but the two are significantly intertwined, as in the process of the Seven Level Outcome Evaluation.

Carpenters say, "Measure twice, cut once." Project managers need to say, "Think many times; then act decisively."

5

When the Project Appears Impossible

This foolish idea of shooting at the moon is an example of the absurd length to which vicious specialization will carry scientists working in thought-tight compartments. Let us critically examine the proposal. For a projectile entirely to escape the gravitation of earth, it needs a velocity of seven miles a second. The thermal energy of a gramme [gram] at this speed is 15,180 calories. . . . The energy of our most violent explosive—nitroglycerine—is less than 1,500 calories per gramme. Consequently, even had the explosive nothing to carry, it has only one-tenth of the energy necessary to escape the earth. . . . Hence the proposition appears to be basically impossible.
—Alexander William Bickerton, Professor of Physics and Chemistry, Canterbury College, Christchurch, New Zealand, 1926

Possible in Theory, Impossible in Practice

Project management may not be exactly rocket science, but it takes advanced creative thinking to break through some of the technical, cognitive, and structural barriers surrounding your project. Take a closer look at the quote that begins this chapter. We obviously know Professor Alexander W. Bickerton is wrong, but if we roll the clock back to 1926 and look at the problem through his eyes, why wouldn't we conclude, as he did, that the "proposition appears to be basically impossible?"

The scientific data Professor Bickerton cites—the thermal energy required to accelerate a gram to a speed of seven miles a second, the energy produced by nitroglycerine—are correct. Nitroglycerine as a fuel would deliver only a tenth of the energy necessary to lift its own mass, much less produce sufficient energy to place a payload in orbit. That's why space travel was a childish fantasy, suitable only for the cover of science fiction magazines (see Figure 5-1).

Imagine yourself in the position of a 1926 project manager asked to go to the moon. How can you manage a project if the project is inherently impossible?

That's a challenge even for the most creative project manager. In this chapter, you'll learn how a creative project manager can sometimes do the impossible—and how to recognize what even the most creative project manager can't.

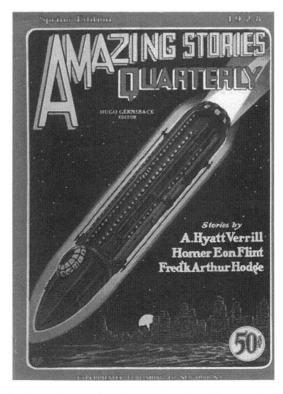

Figure 5-1. Rocketry and space travel was considered impossible by everyone except a small group of eccentrics.

Clarke's Law

Famed science fiction author Arthur C. Clarke offered this principle: "If an elderly and distinguished scientist says something is possible, he is almost certainly right; but if he says it is impossible, he is very probably wrong." Clarke may well have had Professor Bickerton in mind.

Bickerton, Clarke explained, committed two technical errors. The first error was failing to note that the objective is to produce energy, not simply violence, from a rocket fuel. Nitroglycerine contains much less energy per gram than kerosene; it's just much more volatile. Bickerton's second error was assuming the fuel has to carry its own weight into space. It doesn't. The majority of the fuel in a rocket launch is burned very close to the surface of our planet. If nitroglycerine has only a tenth of the energy needed, all that means is that you need 10 pounds of nitroglycerine to launch 1 pound into space.

Professor Bickerton is right that you can't ignore the facts, and he didn't. More important, though, it's the *understanding* of those facts that makes the difference, and again, he did not understand. It is in this point that you can see the relevance for project managers. In project management, the quality of your understanding (or lack thereof) may block you from doing what you want, or it may send your project off into some impossible dimension.

Facts alone aren't enough to correct wrong thinking.

When Your Project Appears Impossible

Just because a project *appears to be* impossible doesn't mean it really *is* impossible. Conversely, just because a project *appears to be* possible doesn't mean it actually *is* possible. Assumptions at both ends of the spectrum carry risk.

Many "impossible" projects are accomplished in spite of initial perceived difficulties. Sometimes the problem that appears at first to be insolvable eventually yields to hard work; other times, avenues that were shrouded in uncertainty open up to reveal new vistas of possibility, as a result of creativity. If there's a way the project could be done, and you don't know what it is, then there's a cognitive bias at work keeping you from seeing it.

There are many possible ways to succeed in managing an "impossible" project:

- Sometimes a team discovers a brilliant critical insight, or it is simply smart enough and good enough to achieve what lesser mortals could not.

- Sometimes the team gets it done by sheer Herculean effort, working harder and longer than anyone expects.

- Sometimes the team gets it done, but at a high price. Maybe the project exceeds one or more of the Triple Constraints, and as a result there's been attrition or long-term damage to the organization.

- Sometimes the team fakes it, slaps a coat of paint on it, and hopes nobody notices that the wheels have fallen off.

That being said, it's important to distinguish between impossible in theory and impossible in practice. We won't argue with the aphorism that nothing's impossible in theory, but for our purposes, we only care about what's possible or impossible under real-world conditions.

In this chapter, we'll learn to identify "impossible" projects operationally, analyze the key issues, pursue a variety of strategies to make the impossible possible, and take the necessary actions to finish — or, if necessary, terminate — the project.

Our four-step cycle for managing impossible projects (see Table 5-1) has parallels in other areas of risk and project management thinking, as well as links to W. Edward Deming's famous Plan-Do-Study-Act (PDSA) cycle.

Table 5-1. Four Steps for Managing Impossible Projects

Impossible Projects	PMBOK Risk Process	Deming PDSA Cycle
Identify What obstacles make the project appear impossible?	**Identify** What risks do we see in our environment?	**Plan** What are the opportunities for improvement?
Analyze What is the structure of the obstacle? What are our constraints?	**Analyze** How serious are they? What are their characteristics?	**Do** Can these improvements be realized profitably? Which should we do first?
Solve What can we do about the obstacles to eliminate the impossibility?	**Develop Response Strategy** Avoid, transfer; mitigate, contingent response; accept	**Study** Develop a plan and benchmarks; implement the solution; study the results.
Finish Implement our solution and finish the project; or decide the project isn't feasible and terminate it.	**Monitor and Control** Has a risk occurred? Is it one we planned for? Does our solution work? Is it time to close the risk?	**Act** Have we achieved the goal? Do we repeat the cycle, abandon the attempt, or move on after success?

What Makes a Project Impossible?

There are many types of impossibility: legal, scientific, metaphysical, and logical, to name a few. Each has its own definition and its own specific context. Our question is more focused: "What does *impossible* mean in the context of project management—and more important, in the context of *your* project (see Table 5-2)?"

Table 5-2. Benchmarks of Impossibility

Model	Definition of Impossibility
Gap Analysis Model	A project that does not appear able to bridge the identified gap sufficiently for a cost less than that of allowing the gap to persist
Basic 3-Level Triage Model	Projects that fall into Category 2: "those that are likely to die, regardless of what care they receive"
Seven Level Outcome Model	A project that will likely achieve outcomes no higher than failure, *regardless of the level of effort,* is impossible. A project that can only achieve levels higher than failure at an *unacceptable cost* is obviously possible, but it's probably not a good idea, so we treat it as impossible for the sake of the process.

Literal, theoretical impossibility isn't required here. Nor is proof that the project will turn out to be impossible after analysis. Our purpose here is deliberately limited to performing a triage on these projects pending subsequent analysis.

What to Say and Do at the Moment of Transition

As Dwight D. Eisenhower's response to George C. Marshall demonstrated, our actions at the moment we receive a project assignment or request can have an outsize impact: the most dangerous action, we've learned, is saying "yes" prematurely.

A good first step in receiving any project assignment or request is to repeat it back, preferably in the same language as you received it. Not only does this tend to reassure the customer that you've heard it, it also gives you time to think about what is the *minimum necessary decision and action right now.*

While saying "yes" prematurely can backfire, you can also get in a world of trouble by being too quick to say "no." Even if your experience and wisdom tell you the project is impossible, saying so too quickly will produce a negative reaction.

When Eisenhower said to Marshall, "Give me a few hours," it was not the mere fact of the delay that mattered. It's what he *did* with those hours. He did some research. He organized his thoughts. He mentally tested his propositions. And he went back with a thorough answer, which almost certainly included a list of some of the major problems and constraints the United States was facing. Some of the news can't have made Marshall happy.

If your project's impossible, or at least compromised, there's still a customer problem needing to be solved. Telling people what they *can* do and what they *can* have tends to get a better reception than telling people what they *can't* do and what they *can't* have. It's important to present alternative options to whoever is depending on you to finish the impossible project.

When you analyze an apparently impossible or potentially impossible project, here's some of what you may learn:

1. You confirm that the project is in fact impossible and can provide evidence to the customer. You and the customer can begin to figure out what alternatives may exist or how to deal with the consequences of an unsuccessful project.
2. You confirm that the project as originally proposed is in fact impossible but are able to find potential changes that will make the project possible, which you can present to the customer.
3. You confirm that the project as stated is in fact impossible but are able to offer alternatives and compromises that might satisfy at least some of the customer's requirements and needs, or close part of the gap.
4. You can't confirm that the project is in fact impossible, but you can identify at least some of the risks and challenges you face, which you and the customer can then assess.
5. You find a creative way around the barrier that makes the project impossible and achieve the original goal.

Even if your analysis leads to the first outcome (it's just flat-out impossible), your situation is still improved by both your ability to give a thoughtful reply with supporting evidence and your attitude in making a good-faith attempt to solve the problem. Partial successes (outcomes 2, 3, and 4) are a marked improvement. Even if the project is impossible—or highly risky—as stated, the customer may be able to get a significant portion of what he or she wants. Plus, it's well known that the first approximation of available constraints may not be the final word. There may be more to draw on. And people tend to react better to hearing what they *can* have and less well to hearing what they *can't* have. The fifth outcome (solve the problem with creativity) is ideal, but often it is challenging and not always successful. The best direction to find the creative answer is, paradoxically, to focus on the barriers in the first place.

Analyzing Your Constraints

Project management impossibility necessarily falls into the envelope of the Triple Constraints. In other words, something is impossible if it cannot be accomplished within the time constraint, within the cost constraint, and to the level specified in the performance criteria. If the Triple Constraints can be modified (or in some cases bypassed or ignored), the project may become possible (see Figure 5-2).

If you suspect that a project may be impossible, the essential first thing to do is to define why it is you think so. In Table 5-3, you'll see questions corresponding to each leg of the Triple Constraints, essentially: "Do we have enough time and enough resources to achieve the mandatory goal?" What's considered "achievable" is usually driven by context. It's easy to build a carbon dioxide filter on Earth; there's a standard specification; a deadline is measured in weeks, if not months; and all the resources you need are easy to acquire. In a crisis situation, such as the one that existed on the Apollo 13 mission, the project looks a little different.

At the beginning of the project, the engineers involved could not know whether the project would turn out to be ultimately impossible. Table 5-3 shows what would have made the project impossible in each dimension of the Triple Constraints.

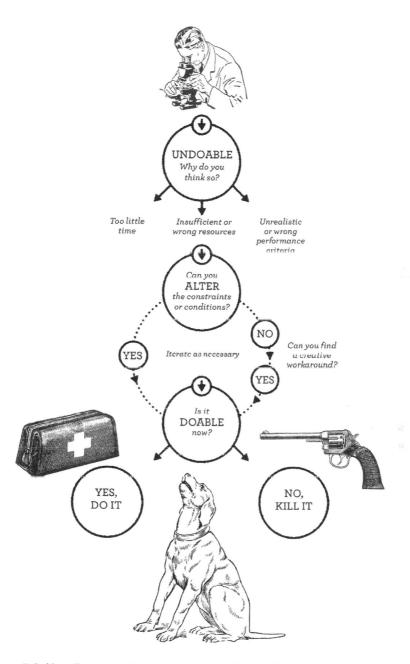

Figure 5-2. Not all proposed projects are possible, but it's not a good idea to conclude this too quickly. Conduct a careful assessment first, but if the project needs to be killed, sooner is generally preferable to later.

Table 5-3. Impossible in Three Dimensions

Constraint	Questions for the Project
Time constraint	**Does the time necessary to accomplish the project exceed the time available?** In developing a replacement for the Apollo 13 mission's overloaded carbon dioxide filter, engineers are constrained by the amount of time until the astronauts became too impaired to build what they designed. If the deadline turns out to be too short, then the project is impossible.
Cost constraint	**Do the resources needed to accomplish the project exceed the resources available?** The project is constrained by what is actually available on the spacecraft. If their resources are short by even one critical component, no matter how small, the project is impossible.
Performance criteria	**Are the performance criteria achievable within the outer boundaries of the other constraints?** If the carbon dioxide filter can't be made to work long enough for the astronauts to reach Earth's orbit when they can return to the command module, then the project is impossible

For Professor Bickerton, cognitive biases about the laws of physics and chemistry falsely created insurmountable barriers to space flight. But insurmountable barriers of the mind are self-imposed, which fortunately only block certain avenues of approach to a solution. Aviators do not and cannot "overcome" the law of gravity; aircraft fly by leveraging other laws in new ways and combinations. Fliers know they're not "overcoming" gravity; if anything, they're far more sensitive to and respectful of the nuances of gravity than those who keep their feet on terra firma.

For our operational discussion, mandatory constraints become part of the definition of *impossible*. It's not impossible in theory to violate a law, a regulation, or an ethical code, but in terms of the practical project management environment, it's usually better to treat such factors as something pretty close to absolutes. There had better be an overwhelmingly good reason for transgression.

On the other hand, taking a detailed look at the law, the regulation, or the ethical code to figure out if legitimate maneuvering room exists is well within the range of appropriate action. Ethics training, for example, often emphasizes the importance of analyzing situations that are complex or ambiguous. What you cannot do one way may be possible to do a different way and still keep you within acceptable limits. But risk is always present.

The fact you can't *do* certain things doesn't mean you shouldn't *talk* about them. A particular project team worried about a company's precarious financial condition conducted a brainstorming session. One participant suggested, "Let's burn down the warehouse for the insurance money!" Obviously, no one—not even the person suggesting it—thought this was a good idea or had any intention of following through. But the facilitator wrote it down on the list of ideas anyway, because in brainstorming you write down all ideas, no matter what.

In the follow-up discussion, "burn down the warehouse" turned into an idea for a "fire sale" of excess merchandise—an ethically and legally appropriate action that accomplished much the same result.

Often, people refer to this as "thinking outside the box."

Thinking Outside the Box

The phrase "thinking outside the box" has its origin in a puzzle known as the Nine Dots, frequently used in management training and consulting since the late 1960s. (It's actually quite a bit older. It seems to have first appeared in Sam Loyd's 1914 *Cyclopedia of Puzzles* as "Christopher Columbus's Egg Puzzle.") Some credit the widespread use of the puzzle to the Walt Disney Company, where it was used in-house to illustrate the power of expanded thinking.

In this puzzle, nine dots are arrayed in a 3×3 pattern, as in the top example of Figure 5-3. Your project is to connect all nine dots in four straight, continuous lines that pass through each dot without lifting your pen or pencil from the paper. It's trivially easy to accomplish the process in five steps, as shown in the second image, but a lot of people are stymied when asked to do it in four lines. They are bounded not only by the constraints of the instructions but also by self-imposed mental limitations. To solve the puzzle in four lines, you have to violate the imaginary boundaries of the area defined by the dots themselves—to *literally* "think outside

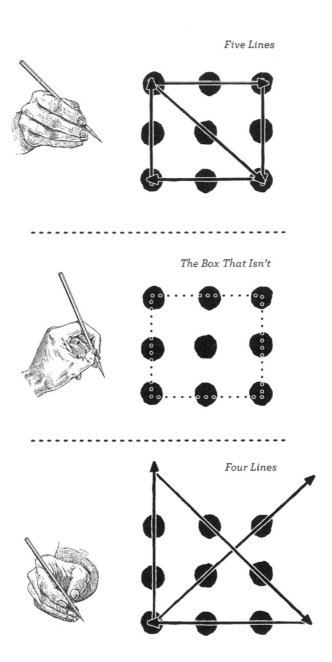

Figure 5-3. The traditional Nine Dots puzzle (Christopher Columbus's Egg Puzzle) showing the four-line solution.

the box," as you see in the figure. Then the impossible becomes possible, as in the bottom image.

But of course that's not exactly right. You aren't really supposed to think "outside" the box—you're supposed to realize that the box *doesn't really exist*. It is an imaginary mental construct imposed by your mind, which has a tendency to see patterns where none exist. To solve the puzzle and, more important, apply this technique to real-world problems, you must recognize that your mind can create imaginary constraints, the result of cognitive bias.

The breakthrough comes when you realize that there is no box. The box is a self-imposed mental constraint.

And only when you realize that there is no box can you find the solution.

This leads us to a four-step model for analyzing our impossible project:

1. Where is the box?
2. What are the borders?
3. Are they real?
4. Are they flexible?

In the first two steps, your goal is to identify as many potential constraints as you possibly can (i.e., do negative brainstorming). Then you test each constraint, seeking to identify those that initially appear to be solid but instead are fuzzily defined, self-imposed (like our imaginary box), or flexible to the extent that trade-offs with other constraints can be useful.

Negative Brainstorming

Willie Sutton was infamous for robbing banks because "that's where the money is." Project managers who question look at the negatives because that's where the problems are. We don't want to wallow in the negative, but we can't afford to pretend it's not there. The negative is whatever it is that stands between us and our attempt to close the gap. We must define it in order to manage it. The technique to help identify and focus on these issues is called "negative brainstorming."

A negative brainstorming process works just like a conventional brainstorming session. Participants offer potential ideas on a specific topic with no criticism or evaluation of ideas or suggestions allowed. The major difference between negative brainstorming and conventional brainstorming is that with the former type the specific topic—and the focus of ideas—is negative. In conventional brainstorming, the focus is on finding creative ways to solve the problem. In negative brainstorming, the focus is on finding all the obstacles, barriers, and events, including internal, external, and self-imposed, that could prevent completion of the project as it is currently defined.

Table 5-4 provides some examples of good questions to get a negative brainstorming session started. For each one, we've taken a project discussed in this book and suggested at least one potentially powerful insight that might come out of a negative brainstorming process.

Table 5-4. Sample Negative Brainstorming Questions

Negative Brainstorming Question	Project	Potential Insight
Why is this project impossible?	Patton	It takes weeks to move an army; if we wait until we find out the enemy's up to something, it will be too late to react quickly.
What are all the things we can't possibly do?	Eisenhower	Telling the head of the Army he'll have to wait a few hours during a crisis situation.
What are all the things others can do that will prevent us from accomplishing this project?	Semmelweis	The other physicians could resist our message, feeling they are accused of crimes they did not intend to commit.
What ideas can we think of that absolutely are not worth trying?	Tylenol	Run advertising to *stop* people from taking our product.
What's the worst possible decision we could make right now?	Sewell Avery	Make the wrong bet on the economy—whether it goes up or down.

What could we do to turn this project into a complete catastrophe?	Ford Pinto	We could ignore or trivialize a safety issue — or try to cover it up.
Why are we doomed to fail?	Apollo 13	There are so many different problems to solve, and failing to solve even one of them will result in failure.

In asking a negative question, the questions are not necessarily accurate descriptors of reality. They don't have to be. What the questions have to do is to correspond to the cognitive biases that keep us from finding a solution. We may not in fact be doomed to fail, but a negative brainstorming exercise on "why are we doomed to fail?" is a powerful way to bring the most serious risks and issues to the surface where the team can deal with them.

Negative questions like the ones in Table 5-4 can be utilized with all sorts of brainstorming processes or techniques. Some approaches include having the participants respond in a round-robin style. Another approach is a simple free-for-all where participants offer ideas randomly. The leader can set a time limit or a target total number of ideas before concluding the process. The important thing is to concentrate on finding all the negative possibilities rather than stop and try to solve the barriers as they are identified during the brainstorming phase of the process.

In negative brainstorming, it's vitally important to encourage participants to offer even the most outrageous possibilities that could negatively impact the project. Our goal is to elevate concerns from the subconscious background into the conscious spotlight of project management, and we can only do that if we recognize what they are in the first place. If people feel criticized for stupid suggestions, the total number of suggestions will go down, including the not-stupid ones. That's why, as in all brainstorming processes the initial phase is to gather ideas, not solve problems or criticize specific contributions.

After completing the negative brainstorming session, the evaluation process begins by taking each negative idea in turn and determining (1) if you can overcome the obstacle, and (2) if so, how. At least some (perhaps most) of the constraints, barriers, and issues you identify will turn out to be both real and solid. That's completely normal. You are looking for the exceptions—which potential impossibility isn't impossible after all. In positive brainstorming, most ideas turn out to be of limited utility, but if you get one winner, it can be a game changer.

In negative brainstorming, if most constraints turn out to be solid, but there are exceptions, the project can go from impossible to possible—occasionally, even to easy—in the blink of an eye.

Looking for Constraints in All the Wrong Places

Let's go back to the Nine Dots puzzle.

Experienced salespeople know that objections from prospective customers are a *good* thing. Customers who don't have objections are usually not interested enough to buy. Customers who are engaged in the discussion, on the other hand, have an interest in buying, if the objection can be satisfied. To satisfy the objection, you have to know what it is, and that's why experienced sales professionals spend a lot of time in the essentially negative process of finding out why customers *don't* want to buy.

When you know the customer's objections, you know what is important to them. You can tailor the features and benefits of the product to the essential needs of the customer. Without understanding objections, you are missing the vital intelligence data to understand what stands between you and the sale. To identify what is really holding you back, routinely ask the question, "What are the barriers or objections to your project's success?"

In the Nine Dots puzzle, a good question is, "Why *can't* we solve this puzzle?" Well, we can't use five lines, the lines have to be straight, the pen or pencil can't leave the paper, and . . . our cognitive bias tells us we can't draw outside the borders. Three of the constraints are binding requirements; one is self-imposed. Discovering—and understanding—that one of the constraints is self-imposed and can be ignored opens the door to a solution.

Most people know the four-line solution already, so let's make the problem a bit more difficult. Can you complete the puzzle using only *three* straight lines, connecting all nine dots, without lifting your pen or pencil from the paper?

The process of finding the solution is similar. You have to ask a question, "Why does this puzzle appear impossible to solve?"

The cognitive bias of focalism, which involves putting too much emphasis on a single piece of information, frequently distorts our thinking. In this case it is an axiom from geometry that can blind our thinking. In geometry, a point is defined as having no volume, no area, and no length—it has no dimension at all. If you draw a straight line, it has to go through the center of the point, because there's nothing *but* center.

But does that really apply in this situation? Not at all. These are *dots*, not points, and pretty big ones as well. There's no requirement or rule that specifies all lines have to pass through the exact center of each dot, as in "The Center Hypothesis" (see Figure 5-4). And since there's no such limiting requirement, that implies that a "knight's move" diagonal as seen in the middle section of the figure is possible . . . and with a little more experimenting, you're likely to find the solution labeled "Three Lines."

Let's make it harder yet. Can you connect all nine dots with only a *single* straight line, without lifting pen or pencil from the paper? Again, we continue our negative brainstorming process. What other constraints can you identify? Well, pen and pencil both imply objects with relatively narrow width, but there are novelty pens and fat Magic Markers that make a wider line. That might lead you to the answer in Figure 5-5, the "Fat Line."

Another constraint is that you have a two-dimensional surface (a flat piece of paper) to work with. But what if you could accordion-fold the paper and draw a single line down the edge? That would allow you to create the "accordion fold" (see Figure 5-5).

Continuing with the flat paper idea, what if you could bend the paper, say by pasting it on a spherical object, like a basketball? You could use a variant of the three-line solution, swoop a single line around and around the non-Euclidean ball, and have the one line solution in "Around the World." When you start to think in terms of the constraints, all sorts of solutions present themselves.

Mapping the Borders of Your Project

Just because a constraint is flexible or even nonexistent doesn't mean you've solved the problem. Discovering the "unconstrained constraint" is only the first step. We've opened new perspectives to explore. Now, we

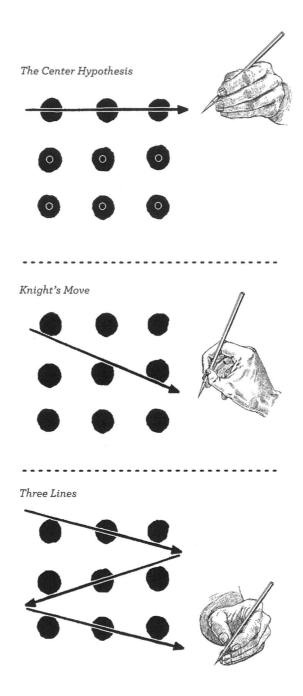

Figure 5-4. You can connect nine dots with three lines if you identify another false constraint: that lines must always go through the center of each dot.

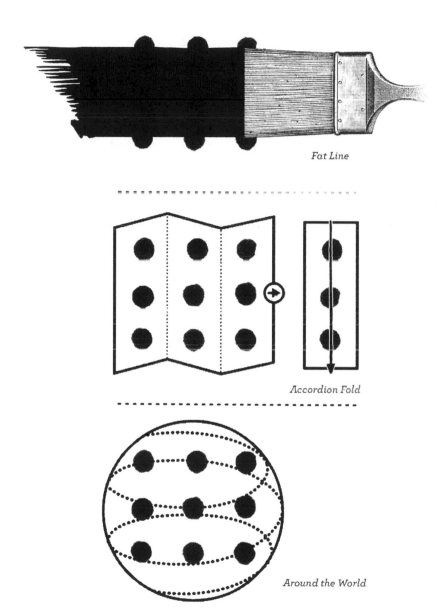

Fat Line

Accordion Fold

Around the World

Figure 5-5. A more difficult variation of the Nine Dots puzzle.

have a new question, "Does our analysis of the flexible or nonexistent constraint reveal a way to make the impossible possible?"

Constraints, operationally, are what stand between you and the completion of a successful project. If you think a given project may be impossible, it's a function of the constraints you perceive. If the constraints (defined as the borders of the perceived box) can be modified, or if parts of it are optical illusions, then you may have new options available. The game has changed.

Most of the traditional tools in the management consultant bag o' tricks can be repurposed in remapping or determining the true borders of your project constraints. A force-field analysis, a modification of the traditional pro-and-con T-chart, illustrates the effect of individual constraints on project objectives, helping you identify the most fertile targets for further exploration. Again, let's use the Apollo 13 carbon dioxide filter project as an example (see Table 5-5).

The current performance or expected outcome (good or bad) is the equilibrium point where current success forces and failure forces balance each other out. To change performance in the direction of more success, you must add new success forces, strengthen success forces already present, eliminate failure forces, or reduce failure forces already present. Your changed performance reflects the new balance point.

Table 5-5. Force-Field Analysis: Apollo 13

Success Forces	Failure Forces
Engineering skill of our team	Limited time available before the astronauts become impaired
Supply of working filters for the command module	Incompatibility of command module filters with lunar module sockets
Ability of astronauts to resist the effects of anoxia	Limits to human ability to resist the effects of anoxia
…	…

How can we change the box defined by our constraints? Logic suggests two possibilities. If the constraints are real and have flexibility, you can change them. If the constraints turn out not to be real, they no longer affect you. Our negative brainstorming process helps you figure out which classification is more appropriate for each constraint.

Depending on what you find, there are multiple strategies to help you with the next step (see Table 5-6).

Table 5-6. Ways to Accomplish an Impossible Project

1. Change the constraints	Analysis
	Negotiation
	Problem solving
	Requirements management
2. Get around the constraints	Creativity
	Exploiting holes
	Different approaches
	Rethinking assumptions

Change the Constraints

While some constraints are mandatory and unbendable, others have substantial flexibility or can be rewritten altogether. Analysis can help you find out which are which. Negotiation, problem solving, and requirements management are the processes by which you can change them.

■ **Analysis.** You have to understand the complete picture to see all the options and just as important, to see all the dangers—that's why it's best to start off with analysis. Why is your preferred option best for the organization? Does your preferred option cause collateral damage elsewhere in the project's environment? How much of this is political? How do other people view this concern? You may sometimes discover that the flexibility in a constraint is buried in the nuances of how other people are affected by it.

■ **Negotiation.** Some constraints are subject to negotiation. If you're bidding on a contract, there's a price at which you can't afford the business. On the other hand, sometimes the organization makes the choice on your behalf: "We've already got the contract, this is the scope of work, and this is how much we can spend to get it done." Probe the constraints to see which are negotiable and which are fixed by circumstances.

Internally, negotiation is the process of making the business case. If you have *force majeure* to settle the argument, it's not really negotiation. In negotiation, being forceful is not an option. You can only win if you are able to help other people recognize and accept a victory of their own.

■ **Problem solving.** You can argue with decisions; you can't argue (though many try) with facts. That's a problem. Some problems, though, can be solved. In the Apollo 13 case we discussed earlier, they needed a particular resource (a filter cover), but there was nothing at hand to do the job. Then someone remembered the astronauts wore socks.

■ **Requirements management.** There is an unfortunate sense in which written requirements too easily turn into Holy Scripture. The purpose of requirements is to define operationally and specifically what the customer wants and wishes to pay for. There's always a delicate balance between imposing the detail necessary for control and allowing the flexibility necessary for exceptional achievement.

Watch out for requirements that have outlived their usefulness or have even become unproductive to the mission. A small change in a requirement may be of little consequence to the project's quality; still, it may spell the difference between success and failure.

Get Around the Constraints

■ **Creativity.** Here is where positive brainstorming rejoins the flow. Systematic creativity—inspiration on time, on budget, and on spec— seems like a contradiction in terms, but professionals in many areas do it as a matter of course. The secret goes back to Thomas Edison's famous ratio of 1 percent inspiration and 99 percent perspiration: creativity is something you can work at. Artists do rough sketches; writers do rough drafts; lightbulb inventors test filament after filament. It's a process of discovery. As the old observation goes, Michelangelo created his *David* by taking a big block of marble and chipping away all the pieces that didn't look like David.

- **Exploiting holes.** People who fish know one trick is to go where the fish are biting. One of the tricks of structured creativity is understanding that some places are more likely to contain insights than others. You should look in those places first. In project management, take a close look at the flexibility of the weak constraint. You may have significant maneuvering room. When you determine the critical path, and identify the presence of slack and float in noncritical activities, there's more flexibility you can use. And, as we've noted, taking a hard look at the constraint itself through negative brainstorming can often lead to discovering places in which it is less constraining.

- **Different approaches.** Insanity, Albert Einstein famously observed, is doing the same thing over and over again and expecting different results. Is there a way around your current obstacle if you switch approaches?

- **Rethink assumptions.** Assumptions can err on the side of optimism or pessimism. Conduct a sensitivity analysis of your assumptions: if it turns out to be true or false, how much impact will it have on your project? Investigate the assumptions with the most potential.

Managing the Impossible Project

Imagine you've been given this as a project objective: "We'd like you to overthrow the foreign government that has dominated your land for the last 190 years. There is no budget, you don't get any staff, and there's no title or authority that comes with your job assignment. No one else has succeeded at this, and some of them had large armies to fight with."

To any sensible person, that's got to be an impossible project. Yet one project manager accomplished exactly that.

In the Battle of Plassey (1757), the British East India Company, aided by bribes and a fortuitous rainstorm that soaked the French artillery's gunpowder, defeated the numerically stronger army of the Nawab of Bengal, the key battle in their campaign to establish British rule in India. For the next 190 years, the British played the "Great Game," becoming an empire on which the sun never sets. Time after time, the British had prevailed over whatever combination of forces threatened their Raj. Their political and military leadership were brilliant.

Indians, on the other hand, were second-class citizens in their own country—signs reading "No Dogs or Indians Allowed" were common in British-patronized shops and restaurants.

A London-educated Indian lawyer named Mohandas K. Gandhi, (see Figure 5-6), who had spent years fighting for Indian civil rights, knew the British had to leave India, but the question was *how*. The constraints appeared overwhelming (see Table 5-7). India was less a nation than a collection of small principalities and fiefdoms, with rulers who worried more about their neighbors than about the British. By playing one off against

Figure 5-6. Mohandas K. Gandhi's law office in Johannesburg, South Africa, 1902. Gandhi spent 20 years protesting the treatment of Indians in South Africa by the British, during which he evolved many of the concepts he used in his later campaigns to free India from British rule.

another, the British had been able to keep any Indian ruler from amassing a force strong enough to defeat them. The British military had more and better weapons—and far better training.

Table 5-7. The Gap and Constraints for Gandhi's Independence Movement

Issue	Description
Gap	Where we are: under domination of a powerful foreign ruler Where we want to be: an independent nation
Cost constraint	No organized military forces, few guns, and little or no money (driver)
Performance constraint	A free, independent, unified India, capable of writing its own destiny in the world (middle constraint)
Time constraint	As soon as possible, but there is no specific deadline (weak constraint)

The Triple Constraints provide the basic framework of the box, but there are other constraints as well. In particular, Gandhi followed the Jainist principle of *ahimsa*, a reverence for all life, and he had a deep commitment to nonviolence. When you add up all the constraints, it's pretty clear that this project is impossible to accomplish.

And yet, Gandhi succeeded.

From any sensible point of view, a single lawyer without political connections had zero chance of defeating the empire on which the sun never set. This is a textbook example of an impossible project becoming possible. Knowing what's at stake and what you're willing to pay is very important when you're tackling a project of great difficulty and uncertain outcome. And, of course, knowing how to analyze and strategize your options is equally essential.

Let's apply our earlier tools to Gandhi's problem. Remember, our options are these: the constraints may be real, in which case we need to see if they can be changed or modified, or they may not be real, in which case we have additional freedom of action. At the beginning of our process, we don't know for sure which situation applies, so we attack the problem from both directions.

Changing the Constraints

If the constraints are real but could potentially be flexible, Gandhi needs to look for ways to change the constraints (see Table 5-8).

Table 5-8. Changing the Constraints

Tool	Options
Analysis	Gandhi no doubt understands the problem in broad outline from the outset, but mastery only comes through study and analysis. Getting a more complete picture can be depressing in the short run, but illuminating and transformational in the long run.
Negotiation	In this case, Gandhi is not empowered yet to negotiate with the British. He might be able to negotiate small-scale adjustments, but these would not solve his problem. However, it's important to note that negotiation would be part of any end-game strategy, so it's wise to think about what you want before someone asks you.
Problem solving	The size and dimension of the problem, at first glance, suggests it's unlikely Gandhi can tackle it directly. He doesn't have the strength. If there's an answer to his problem, it will have to involve some sort of leverage, something indirect.
Research	In the process of turning a dream into a reality (which gives birth to a project), you have to study the situation. Who are the stakeholders? What forces are arrayed against you? Who can help? What are the strengths and weaknesses of each side?

Getting Around the Constraints

If the constraints are potentially not real, or are not equally constraining in all directions, Gandhi needs to figure out possible ways to get around them or make them vanish (see Table 5-9).

Table 5-9. Getting Around the Constraints

Tool	Options
Creativity	Is there new technology, or a new strategic breakthrough, that would provide the necessary strength to overturn British rule?
Exploiting holes	Exploiting rivalries and playing one side against the other is the fundamental British strategy; force of arms comes into play when strategy fails. Could this strategy be reversed and used against the British? Are there British allies who could be peeled away?
Different approaches	One can counter a military occupation with military tactics, but are there other approaches, such as economic or political, that might be successful?
Rethink assumptions	Through negative brainstorming, consider all the ways the problem *can't* be solved, and see if any of those barriers yield to closer examination.

Still More Project Questions

In searching for some kind of creative solution to this project, there are several more questions the Indians could ask themselves that might point the way toward an answer:

1. What's our biggest weakness? (Too few guns compared to our enemy)
2. What's the best and finest quality of our enemy? (A belief in their own goodness)
3. What's the craziest thing we could do? (Going up against armed soldiers with flowers might qualify)
4. What cognitive biases do we and our opponents have that might create blind spots? (There's a wide assortment to choose from, and each may create opportunities.)

One strategy the creative project manager can use is the search for apparent paradoxes. In this case, Gandhi has a strong commitment to peace and nonviolence, and yet what the situation calls for is a successful war. With that in mind, let's revisit our earlier discussion of Carl von Clausewitz. We don't know whether Gandhi read Clausewitz or not, but thinking about war is a particularly valuable tool for someone devoted to peace. War is a way to achieve your ends by imposing your will on that of your opponent. You conduct a war when you cannot get what you want through negotiation and when the situation is completely unacceptable. The situation for Indians in the British Raj, as far as Gandhi was concerned, was unacceptable and did not seem to yield to negotiation.

The first step to imposing your will on your adversaries is to deprive them of their weapons. The British had more and better weapons than the Indians. The British also considered themselves morally and racially superior, and therein lies an opportunity. If the Indians fought, the British could shoot them. But if the Indians ostentatiously eschewed the use of violence, it would be progressively more difficult for the British to use their military might. World opinion and the British own sense of moral superiority both worked against them. By refusing to use the relatively few guns on the Indian side, Gandhi forced the British to put aside a far greater number of guns.

This is the heart of Gandhi's philosophy of *satyagraha*, which he defined as resistance to tyranny through mass civil disobedience, with a commitment to total nonviolence. Make no mistake, however: this was war. The British had no intention of abandoning the "Jewel in the Crown." It took force—in this case, moral force—to bring them to the negotiating table.

From one point of view, Gandhi conducted a war—a nonviolent one—against the British. His ideas didn't come to him overnight but as the result of substantial thinking and various early false starts. At no time was his mission easy, and he experienced many reversals in his long fight for Indian independence. Ultimately, the project cost him his life.

But he succeeded.

How to Terminate a Doomed Project

At some point, you and your team will have tried everything you know how to try. Sometimes a project really needs to die, and the project manager is often the one dispatched to do the dirty deed. The constraints that prevent success cannot be changed and cannot be evaded by any means. Even if it turns out there's an answer that's been missed, at this point you're stuck. The choice is to try to get the project killed up front or to let the customer spend all that time and money only to end up with inevitable failure.

Fortunately, this termination process is often quite straightforward. You present your analysis, gain stakeholder agreement, and shut down the project in an orderly manner. (The creative project manager's approach to closeout gets covered in Chapter 10.) At other times, the process involves risk—which, as you know, includes opportunity as well as threat.

So far in this book, we have discussed some of the better known disasters in project management. Few are more famous than the automated baggage handling system at Denver International Airport (DIA), which burned through $250 million before being abandoned as unworkable. There's nothing inherently impossible about the concept of an automated baggage handling system, though obviously the implementation is tougher than it appears. No, this is the kind of project in which impossibility is situational: a function of the constraints. While we've focused on the Triple Constraints because of their universal application in project management, individual projects have other constraints as well.

The airlines themselves, oddly, had little initial involvement in the airport planning. This gave them substantial leverage later in the process. "If you build it, they will come" often carries a hefty price tag. In order to keep its costs down, United Airlines needed the baggage transfer system to take no longer than 45 minutes to route luggage among its flights.

In 1992, the automated baggage handling system was shoehorned into existing construction in what amounted to a "Hail Mary" play. In terms of project scope, the engineering involved was a great leap forward from third-generation to sixth-generation technology. Performance, obviously, was the project driver, with budget unavoidably the weak constraint. Significant cost and schedule overruns were guaranteed, and to a large extent they were acceptable—as long as performance goals were achieved.

So far, we have a very challenging project, but there's no reason for a project manager to propose killing it. It's not operationally impossible, and the value of closing the gap justifies a very high level of effort.

The project team developing the automated baggage handling system, BAE Systems, officially recognized these key risks:

- Very large scale of the project

- Enormous complexity

- Newness of the technology

- Large number of entities to be served by the system

- High degree of technical and project definition uncertainty

The most important risk, however, was not mentioned: the complex stakeholder environment. The initial project was originally intended simply to serve United Airlines. DIA management expanded the contract to cover all terminals. DIA rejected the BAE proposal to build a 50,000-square-foot prototype. Scheduling issues with other construction activities caused huge conflict.

There's the old story about the two frogs who fell into pots of water. One pot had hot water, and the frog immediately jumped out. The other pot was warming slowly, so the other frog felt no urgency about escaping until it was too late.

BAE was the second frog.

The cognitive bias at work here is *déformation professionnelle*, the tendency to see everything through the eyes of your own profession. Because the project is not impossible from an engineering perspective, the fact that it is becoming operationally impossible because of the constraints of the stakeholder environment tends to escape notice until it's too late.

On the other hand, political problems aren't exactly unknown. Project managers are supposed to perform a stakeholder analysis. This isn't just about figuring out your customers—it's about analyzing the political landscape.

The Godzilla principle reminds us that the earlier we identify a risk or problem, the more options are available. If you accompany the sales team when bidding on a job, don't confine yourself to a study of the technical issues. As project manager, you're going to have to spend your days dealing with the people, and you can't tell the players without a scorecard. If you detect political dangers, they need to be part of your risk analysis for the job, as they will affect pricing and schedule. This undertaking ought to be done not just for your sake as project manager but also for the sake of the entire job.

If you get into the job and find that these issues are getting out of control, you likely don't have the power to get out of the problem by yourself. You need allies, and you need them to figure out the problem for themselves. Most project managers see reporting (no matter how necessary) as something that takes time away from doing the work. Reporting, however, is a strategic tool to lay the information groundwork with your stakeholder community to bring them toward the correct understanding of the real situation.

The best way to kill a project is to help the key stakeholders and decision makers reach the conclusion on their own rather than you telling them. Remember that "operationally impossible" means *you* can't figure out an answer. Leave open the possibility that someone else might have an answer you've missed. Sometimes they do have an answer for you. And if they don't, they are more likely to agree with your assessment.

Sometimes canceling a project is peaceful; sometimes it's a mess. The DIA baggage system project ended with mutual lawsuits. That's a powerful argument for acting early when the project is likely to be operationally impossible.

6

Knowns and Unknowns:
The Risk Factor

The revolutionary idea that defines the boundary between
modern times and the past is the mastery of risk: the notion that
the future is more than a whim of the gods and that men
and women are not passive before nature.
—Peter L. Bernstein, *Against the Gods:*
The Remarkable Story of Risk (1998)

What Is Risk?

A risk is a proposed future event that would have a significant impact on you or on something you care about if it should happen. The effect may be negative (a threat) or positive (an opportunity), but the outcome won't be revealed until the event actually occurs. Risk, above all, involves uncertainty. That's how we distinguish a risk from a problem: a problem is certain.

We often manage risk by denial, declaring ourselves helpless in the face of implacable destiny or checking our horoscope to find a propitious day to ask for that promotion. We deny the existence of randomness by chanting self-help mantras—"I'm good enough, I'm smart enough, and doggone it, people like me!"—declaring ourselves solely responsible for all that befalls us.

There is, however, a science of risk. We tend to notice the work of risk professionals only when it results in failure—for example, when the patchwork of convertible debt swaps backing subprime mortgages unravels due to faulty risk pricing. But it's not only the economy, stupid. Risk managers keep airplanes in the air, stop buildings from collapsing, and secure every bit of a modern infrastructure. Taking risks—the right risks— is necessary. Thoughtful and creative risk management is essential.

Probability and Impact

How likely is it that a risk will occur? You have to take into account both the severity of the impact and its likelihood. Sometimes we know with mathematical certainty whether a risk will occur. More often than not, the best we can do is guess at the likelihood of something happening— whether it's quite low or almost certain. Impact can sometimes be turned into a number, say, $1,000, or €50. Other times, it's about as ill defined as that scene in *Ghostbusters* when Egon explains what will happen if they cross the energy streams of their proton packs: "It would be bad."

The standard risk formula is $R = P \times I$ (Value of a risk = Probability $\times$ Impact). That's particularly helpful in pricing financial risk. If there's a 10 percent chance of something happening that would cost you $1,000, then the value of the risk is $100. That means that if you can get rid of the risk for under $100, it's clearly profitable to do so. If it will cost more than $100 to get rid of the risk, you have to consider whether other factors justify the additional cost.

Different Kinds of Risk

Not all risks are created equal, as you'll see in the following paragraphs.

Pure Risk and Business Risk

Because risks can be threats or opportunities, you have to know the difference between a "pure risk" and a "business risk."

A *pure risk* is all downside. Getting into a traffic accident, having your house catch on fire, or losing your wallet are, we hope, unlikely to happen, but they are risks. If they happen, your life gets worse. If these things don't happen, your life doesn't improve; instead, it stays the same. That's a pure risk—all threat, no opportunity. Clearly, avoiding pure risk, if you can do so at an acceptable cost, is a good idea.

A *business risk*—a stock market investment, for example—has an upside and a downside. There is a possibility you will make money, but there's also a possibility you will lose it. The risk formula's $P \times I$ has to be determined for the upside and for the downside, so you can see how the risks balance. If the result is favorable, that's an argument for the investment; if it's unfavorable, perhaps not.

For example, let's say you're offered an investment for $5,000. In return, you are guaranteed a 70 percent chance of making $50,000 and a 30 percent chance of losing your investment. Using the $R = P \times I$ formula, you first calculate the value of the opportunity risk (70% × $50,000 = $35,000) and then the value of the loss (30% × –$5,000=–$1,500). To determine the "estimated monetary value" of the investment, add the values together: $35,000 + (–$1,500) = $33,500.

The estimated monetary value is a type of weighted average. If you made the same investment over and over, winning and losing at the stated values, over time, you'd end up earning $33,500 as an average per investment.

But if you only get to make the investment a single time, you won't get $33,500. You'll either receive $50,000 or lose $5,000. That gives you three possible choices:

1. Bet the upside (in this case, go for the $50,000 payday).
2. Hedge the downside (in this case, don't make the investment to avoid the chance of losing $5,000).
3. Weigh the decision (in this case, you lean toward the investment because the estimated monetary value is much higher than the amount at risk).

Your personal choice may be influenced by how much is in your bank account.

Residual Risk and Secondary Risk

Residual risk is risk left over after you've applied your risk reduction strategies. Most risk strategies can't get rid of every bit of risk. You can come up with additional ways to reduce the residual risk further, but at some point you normally accept some level of residual risk and move on. We take our lives in our hands every day we get behind the wheel of a car, but really, what choice do most of us have?

Secondary risk is new risk created by your proposed solution to the original risk. If you spend time and energy to get rid of Problem A, that means you pay less attention to Problem B, so it's possible you will make things worse overall. Make sure you inspect any proposed solutions for secondary risk before rushing to implement them. We will discuss residual and secondary risk in further detail later in this chapter.

Risk Management Processes

The *PMBOK Guide* approach to risk management forms a solid base for the questioning project manager. We particularly applaud the PMBOK's focus on opportunity risk, too often overlooked in the search for ways to improve your project's performance.

The standard PMBOK risk management model starts with a five-phase process for risk management, shown in Table 6-1. Notice that good risk managers do a lot of analysis before they reach the step of actually figuring out what to do about the risk. If you don't understand the context, you can't very well make the best decision.

Table 6-1. Standard Project Risk Management Processes

Stage	Definition	Strategies
Risk management planning	How are we going to do risk management on this project?	On some projects, you decide on an ad hoc basis; on others, you set up a standard procedure. You can find generic plans on the Internet or hire experts to write and implement them. If you want a standard process, you'll have to train users.
Risk identification	What are the risks on this project?	Brainstorming, lessons learned, expert opinion, research. Err on the side of inclusion. Even if only one or two people think it matters, add it to the list.
Risk analysis	What can we learn about these risks?	Risk triage, assessment of probability and impact, characteristics of risk, possible triggers or circumstances all help you determine the overall risk level of the project.
Risk response planning	What are we going to do about the risks?	There are a limited number of risk management strategies. We'll spell them out later on.
Risk monitoring and control	What's actually happening with the risks?	Triggers, implementing risk responses, closing finished risks, verifying effectiveness of strategies, coming up with new plans, and dealing with surprises.

As you identify and analyze your risks, you end up with a list of prioritized risks that require some sort of action on your part. There are only a finite number of things you can do with a risk. Table 6-2 lists what you can do in response to the most important negative risks (i.e., threats) that face your project.

Table 6-2. Standard Responses to Threat Risks

Threat Strategies	Definition
Avoidance	Changing the project to eliminate the threat altogether (probability = o) or protect the project from its effects (impact = o). There's no residual risk; there may be secondary risk.
Transfer	Moving the threat ownership to someone outside the project: insurance, contract terms, or passing the buck. Not all threat can usually be transferred; residual risk remains. Secondary risk is possible.
Mitigation	Reducing, but not eliminating, some combination of probability (> o) and impact (> o). There's always residual risk; there may be secondary risk.
Contingent response	A risk response that will be triggered only if the threat looks like it's occurring or about to occur. It may involve elements of any other strategy; it may have residual and secondary risk.
Acceptance	No action or planning takes place unless the threat actually occurs. It may involve elements of any other strategy; it may have residual. There's no secondary risk unless the threat occurs.

As we've noted, risks can also have an upside. Business risks, remember, contain both threat and opportunity in a single package. There are also pure opportunities in which you gain a benefit if they happen, and don't experience a loss if they don't happen. Table 6-3 lists the traditional set of responses to opportunity risk.

Table 6-3. Responses to Opportunity Risk

Opportunity Strategies	Definition
Exploitation	Taking the value of the opportunity and using it for the benefit of the project, the customer, or the sponsoring/ performing organization
Sharing	Giving, selling, or trading the value of the opportunity to someone who can potentially derive greater benefit from it
Enhancement	Continuing to invest or grow the value of the opportunity so it will be greater in the future
Contingent response	A risk response that will be triggered only if the opportunity presents itself
Acceptance	No action or planning taking place unless we discover that an opportunity has occurred

Nothing stops you from implementing multiple solutions to the same risk. Contingent responses frequently serve as backup plans to other strategies. Sometimes a single mitigation strategy isn't enough, so you might nibble away at the risk by implementing more than one solution.

Sometimes, however, the situation gets a bit more complicated.

Knowns and Unknowns

The biggest reason for poor risk management is lack of attention and effort in the first place, but sometimes even when you put the work in, there are still problems:

- You may not know enough to identify, much less manage, the risk.

- You may not have the tools or resources, or they may not even exist.

- The risk may be *inequitable*: the secondary impact of the solution may be worse than the primary impact of accepting the risk in the first place.

While risk involves uncertainty, the degree of knowledge about the nature of the risk, its probability, and its impact can vary. That's why the universe of project risk stretches across the spectrum of both known and unknown (see Figure 6-1):

- Known knowns (things that we know that we know)

- Known unknowns (things that we know that we don't know)

- Unknown unknowns (things that we don't know that we don't know)

- Unknown knowns (things that we don't know that we do know)

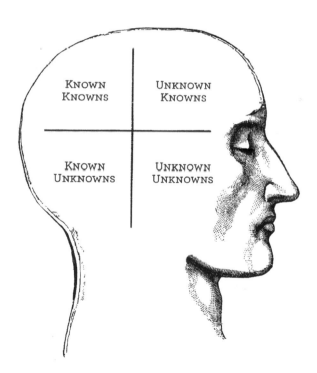

Figure 6-1. The universe of project risk encompasses both knowns and unknowns, shown here as a grid. The art and discipline of risk management has tools to help in all four areas.

The concept of known and unknown risks has echoes in writings from Confucius to Thoreau. Helmuth von Moltke the Elder's adage, "no battle plan survives first contact with the enemy," recognizes the reality of unknown unknowns. And there's a fairly well known principle codified in 1949 by a U.S. Air Force captain Edward Murphy, a development engineer at Edwards Air Force Base, which states that "everything that can go wrong, will." Risk managers know well how easy it is to be blindsided.

Strategies for Managing Knowns and Unknowns

As you go through the permutations of known and unknown, it's important to remember that *risk* is not automatically synonymous with *helplessness*. However, it's seldom the case that the right approach is to ignore the source and nature of risks in the first place. Table 6-4 shows some strategies for dealing with each factor.

Table 6-4. Strategies for Managing Knowns and Unknowns

Category	Definition	Strategies
Known knowns	Definite knowledge of risk, probability, and impact	Safety planning Classical risk management
Known unknowns	Knowledge of risk, fuzzy or nonexistent knowledge of probability, potential wide range of impact	Classical risk management Project risk management
Unknown unknowns	No knowledge of potential risk event, no ability to assess probability, unknown or widely variable impact	Thinking backward Creation and management of reserves Work harder
Unknown knowns	Cognitive biases and assumptions that blind decision makers to available information on potential risk event, probability, or impact	Assumptions analysis Outcome evaluation Negative brainstorming

Known Knowns

Let's imagine we're planning our company's summer picnic for about a hundred people, including employees and family members. We're putting together our project plan, and one element we have to cover, obviously, is risk management. Let's look at potential risk areas in each of the four quadrants, starting with the stuff everyone *knows* is going to happen, our "known knowns" (see Table 6-5).

Table 6-5. Known Knowns

Risk	Response
The kids will get cranky around three o'clock.	Schedule activities and games for the kids in the afternoon, and have lots of supervision.
There will be a few minor cuts and scrapes among the picnickers.	Set up a first aid tent.
Somebody will drink too much.	Establish and enforce liquor rules, and have a backup response to use when those rules are violated.

As we discussed, the classic risk formula $R = P \times I$ (risk equals probability times impact) measures the severity of risk. If the risk formula produces a dollar number, it also serves as a guideline for how much you should spend. If there's a 50 percent risk of losing $1,000, the risk is worth $500. If you spend $900 to mitigate the risk, you were probably better off accepting the risk.

When the probability of the risk trends toward certainty ($P = 100$ percent, $R = I$), the risk enters the realm of known known. Some risks we simply *know* will happen, even if we do not know every detail about it. On a long contract, there will be change orders. If you're managing a network of hundreds of computers, some of them will be down at any given moment.

It's enough to call it a known known if you know enough to develop a strategy for a response. If the cost of the response is less than the cost of suffering the problem, there's a presumption in favor of active response. Project managers need to list known known risks so they don't overlook them.

But what do you do when you know something *might* happen but don't know whether it *will?* That takes us to the next category, known unknowns (see Table 6-6).

Known Unknowns

Table 6-6. Known Unknowns

Risk	Probability (*P*) Impact (*I*)	Possible Responses
It might rain.	*P*: Check weather history. Are we in Seattle or Phoenix? *I*: Eliminates outdoor games	Have a tent; have a rain date; rent a pavilion; have indoor games ready just in case.
Someone might be seriously hurt.	*P*: Low, perhaps very low *I*: Serious, potentially fatal	Investigate the cost of hiring a nurse or paramedic to set up and manage a first aid tent. Make sure there's enough cell-phone reception to call for an ambulance, if you need to; determine the closest hospital and transit time; know the route, and have a vehicle ready.

Known unknowns fall into the domain of classical risk. In the case of known knowns, probability is on the close order of 100 percent. But in known unknowns, probability enters the decision-making sphere. Classical risk management is based on the law of large numbers. A creation of famous mathematicians of the eighteenth century, classical risk is based on statistics. We don't know if your house will burn down, but in a pool of 100,000 houses, we can make a pretty good prediction about how many houses will. In many ways, classical risk management is at the heart of modern economic civilization. From insurance to interest rates, the ability to analyze and measure risk is essential. (At the root of the economic crisis of 2008 and beyond is the unfortunate fact that risk analysts sometimes get it wrong.)

In project management, on the other hand, you often have little or no basis for assessing probability. At best, you can only report a vague feeling for the range. Even if the information is poor, however, don't try to get ahead of your data. Even vague or approximate information (see Table 6-7) can be useful.

Table 6-7. Degree of Knowledge

Accuracy	Probability	Impact	Risk Score ($P \times I$)
Complete	43%	$157,500	$67,725
Substantial	Less than 50%	Between $100,000 and $200,000	Between $50,000 and $100,000
Fuzzy	Moderate	High, depending on the total size of the project and availability of resources	High
Low/none	Unknown	Unknown or situational	Unknown

Until the answers sink completely into the cloud of unknowability, they still provide value. That's why a number of project risk management techniques use fuzzy measurements for risk classification.

We don't really know what the chances are that someone at the picnic will be seriously hurt. Experience suggests that the probability is low, but that does not translate into a business case number. From an operational perspective, however, we are not helpless. When numbers are fuzzier, you have to work a little harder to justify certain decisions. There's nothing wrong with that. As long as we have enough information to allow us to prepare a proportional response, it's absolutely good enough.

Sewell L. Avery, the one-time chairman of Montgomery Ward whom you'll remember from Chapter 2, might have seen it the same way, if he had been able to peer into the postwar future. From the perspective of a planner, Avery needed to act *as if* the postwar economy was in fact both booming and crashing at the same time. Not knowing the truth, he could not afford to be caught short with whatever hand reality eventually dealt him. Alas, he didn't see it that way. He prepared for the threat but not the opportunity—in short, he saw pure risk where he needed to have seen business risk.

All this assumes, of course, that you do know what the possibilities are. Sometimes that's not the case. You not only don't know *whether* a given event might happen, you don't even know *what* the events might be!

In the risk area of unknown unknowns (see Table 6-8), we are feeling our way in the dark.

Unknown Unknowns

Table 6-8. Unknown Unknowns

Risk	Probability (P) Impact (I)	Potential Responses
Unknown	P: Unknown I: Affects our schedule	How much of a deficiency can we tolerate without action? What's the biggest deficiency we can possibly make up? What could we speed up or eliminate from our project in order to make up serious deficiencies in our schedule?
Unknown	P: Unknown I: Affects our budget	How much of a deficiency can we tolerate without action? What's the biggest deficiency we can possibly make up? Where could we cut costs from our project in order to make up serious deficiencies in our budget and resources?
Unknown	P: Unknown I: Affects our performance	How much of a deficiency can we tolerate without action? What's the biggest deficiency we can possibly make up? What could we modify, improve, fix, or eliminate from our project in order to make up serious deficiencies in our performance?

The textbook definition of unknown unknowns refers to any circumstance or event that someone didn't think of at the time. Of course, when it comes to lessons learned, the question becomes not "did you think of it?" but rather "should you have?"

There are four potential strategies to manage unknown unknown risks:

1. Work harder/dig deeper.
2. Think backward.
3. Keep something in reserve.
4. Wait.

Work harder/dig deeper. While it's unrealistic to expect that you can eliminate the set of unknown unknowns completely from any project, reducing the size of the set is normally within your power. The difference between an explanation and an excuse is that an excuse actually absolves the failure. That's why there aren't many excuses but there's always an explanation.

The explanation of any failure is of keen interest to project managers; that's the reason for doing lessons learned at the end of a project. Taking the need for excuse and forgiveness out of the equation is an important tool to make sure the discussion of the root cause is candid and productive.

Thinking backward. Even when the universe of unknown unknowns is practically infinite, there are still common characteristics to hold onto. Any risk event can do only three things to your project: it can make you late (or early), it can drive your cost up (or down), or it can degrade (or enhance) your performance. That means you need three generic strategies to mitigate threats (recover time, recover cost, fix defects) and three to exploit opportunities (decrease time, lower cost, improve quality). Even though you still don't know what might happen, you've got a raft to brave the sea of unknown troubles.

Keep something in reserve. Military planners do not, as a rule, put all their forces on the front lines. Knowing that "no battle plan survives first contact with the enemy," they plan for the plan breaking down. In project management, you have the potential for reserves in the three dimensions of the Triple Constraint: you can have some extra funds for contingencies, some extra time, or some optional scope.

Wait. The last fundamental concept of unknown unknowns is that they are unknown *at some specific moment in time*. We might not be aware of any hazards on the softball field until we get there—but if someone happens to see a broken beer bottle in the dirt at first base, the potential risk profile of the project has changed. The unknown unknown fog has lifted, and now a risk once hidden is visible. If there's still potential information out there, and a decision is not needed right this very moment, waiting can be a very useful strategy.

Most discussions of risk management end here, but when project managers do "lessons learned" on a project, they discover an entirely new category: we knew it, we understood it—but we didn't take action for whatever reason. Worse, we often draw a veil of cognitive bias over the area, so we can't easily see what we're looking for.

That's the risk area of unknown knowns (see Table 6-9), where our own blind spots stand in the way.

Unknown Knowns

Table 6-9. Unknown Knowns

Risk	Why Is It an Unknown Known?
The bad news about the company might get out.	It can't happen. There's no way. None.
The vice president's drinking problem will get out of control again.	The vice president is powerful and vindictive. Nobody's going on record.
There's a big patch of poison ivy around those bushes where the hide-and-seek game is planned.	The head of the site committee doesn't know what poison ivy looks like.

Psychoanalytic philosopher Slavoj Žižek described unknown knowns as that which we don't know or intentionally refuse to acknowledge that we know. We may refuse to pay official notice to that which has no official existence, like office politics. Our corporate values of teamwork and fair play deny the possibility that not everyone is necessarily on board. We give lip service to some corporate values and enforce others ruthlessly. It's certainly true that some things cannot be spoken aloud, but that doesn't mean they cannot be identified or managed.

Risk and the Project Environment

The severity of a risk, whether threat or opportunity, is modified by its context. In our earlier example in which you invested $5,000 for a 70 percent chance at a $50,000 payoff, we noted that financial gain and loss isn't always reciprocal: if you need the $5,000 for food and shelter, the economic consequence of losing the money would be disastrous, no matter how nice it would be to have the $50,000. But to Bill Gates, even *winning* the $50,000 is trivial.

Risks to the project objectives are always serious. But how you classify and look at individual risks is influenced not only by the actual impact but by where in the project environment the impact takes place (see Table 6-10).

Notice that a single risk may have consequences for more than one impact area. The gas tank on the Pinto was a low-impact risk within the Triple Constraints universe of the project (i.e., get the Pinto into production and on the market), but its collateral impact on Ford as an organization was high indeed.

Table 6-10. Areas of Risk Impact

Risk Impact Area	Definition	Typical Impact
Triple Constraints	Risks that would impact cost, time, and performance on the project itself	Influenced by the hierarchy of constraints
Collateral damage	Risks that would damage the organization, delay or destroy other projects, or damage anyone's careers or personal interests	Influenced by the relative value of the projects or interests; also, the relative power of stakeholders with conflicting interests
Intentional damage	Risks that would preempt competitor plans, win market share, or acquire new businesses	Influenced by the goal of the project or interests of the organization
Opportunity	Risks that might provide potential payoffs that we could exploit, share, or enhance	Influenced by value of the opportunity, cost of the opportunity, and collateral damage
Environmental	Risks that would violate the rules or boundaries of our environment— may be illegal, unethical, poor business practice, bad manners, nonstandard procedures, broken industry norms, broken safety rules, or running afoul of the laws of nature	Influenced by the nature and authority of the rule, severity of and likelihood of consequences, personal values of stakeholders, and potential benefit of breaking the rule

Managing Residual and Secondary Risk

Risk that falls outside the Triple Constraints area is still part of the sphere of project risk. Limiting a discussion of risk to its impact on the project objectives puts dangerous blinders on the process.

As we've noted, most risk management strategies have two by-products:

1. *Residual risk*, the risk left over after you've applied your risk response strategy, which may be highly localized
2. *Secondary risk*, new risk created by your risk response, which is not necessarily located in the same place as the original risk

Residual Risk

If you rent a tent in case of rain on your picnic, you've mitigated the impact of the rain risk, but you haven't limited it altogether. Yes, the tent keeps people from becoming soaked, but the softball game can't be saved. When residual risk drops beneath a certain threshold, it makes sense to accept the remaining risk and move on. But look closely. Sometimes the risk strategy has completely eliminated one aspect of a risk and left another completely untouched, which can sometimes mislead the team into thinking the risk has been completely avoided.

There's also a sense of inevitability about residual risk that isn't always accurate. There is no rule in risk management that you have to have one—and only one—strategy per risk. You can have a rain date *and* a tent; you can *also* have backup activities to replace any washed-out events. Sometimes multiple solutions to a single risk can be cheaper and easier than finding and implementing a single Grand Solution.

The level of residual impact can also turn out to be greater than anticipated, especially if the risk is triggered by some underlying environmental condition—a "perfect storm" scenario.

Secondary Risk

Secondary risk is new risk created by your proposed solution to the old risk. That tent we rented costs so much we can no longer afford beer. Clearly, if the secondary risk outweighs the primary risk, it makes sense to look for a different solution. Before you do, however, it may be worthwhile to see if the proposed solution can be modified to reduce or eliminate the secondary risk.

The practice of medicine often requires extraordinary focus on secondary risk. Surgery, prescription drugs, and all sorts of treatment carry inherent risks of their own, which must be compared against the risk of the original condition. A higher dosage might be desirable for treating the disease but less desirable for the rest of the body. Sometimes a physician will choose an alternate course of treatment; other times, the right decision is to accept the secondary risk and proceed.

Risk and the Triple Constraints

Within any project, the interplay of time, cost, and performance necessarily turns into a hierarchy of driver, middle, and weak constraint. The reason why we're doing the project in the first place tells us how to triage, the serious question behind the old adage, "Did you want it good, fast, or cheap? Pick two."

The driver is whichever leg of the triple constraints has the least flexibility; the weak constraint has the most. For example, in a cave-in, the time you have to rescue the trapped miners is a strict function of the air available (even if you don't know how much there is). Time is the driver. If the rescue tunnel allows entry to only three workers at a time, it doesn't matter much how many workers are available. Cost is the middle constraint. The only place where flexibility can help is in performance—working harder, refreshing workers more often, bringing in tools, taking greater risks.

You have to meet the driver, or else your project fails. Look at the weak constraint as a place to find help: what kind of flexibility exists, and how can you exploit or leverage it?

The six dimensions of project management (see Table 6-11) are the six different permutations of time, cost, and performance as driver, middle, and weak constraints.

Table 6-11. Six Dimensions of Project Management

Dimension	Hierarchy of Constraints Issues
Time/cost/ performance	There's a deadline after which the project is moot or loses value. Resources at hand and available to work are limited. Often there is a crisis environment. It may be a good idea to target a performance level of barely adequate.
Time/ performance/ cost	There's a deadline after which the project is moot or loses value. The minimum standard for an acceptable outcome is high. Often there is a crisis environment. Look for all possible resources you can exploit; pour as much as you can into the job.
Performance/ time/cost	The performance target is challenging but necessary (or at least highly desirable). There's a strong source of time pressure, perhaps a race to market. The value of the performance is high enough to justify extra resources; use them.
Performance/ cost/time	The performance target is challenging but necessary (or at least highly desirable). Key resources are limited or unavailable. While there may be an overall sense of urgency, the project will still be desirable even if it is late.
Cost/time/ performance	Key resources are limited or unavailable, or there's huge demand for the same resources by multiple projects with high priorities. Time is limited, but it is more flexible than cost. Performance levels of barely adequate may constitute an acceptable outcome.
Cost/ performance/ time	Key resources are limited or unavailable, or there's huge demand for the same resources by multiple projects with high priorities. If the desired quality of performance is not achieved, the value of the finished project will be degraded or destroyed. Stretching out the project over a longer time frame may allow funding to continue.

In risk management, thinking about the Triple Constraints reveals a new set of risk response strategies (see Table 6-12).

Table 6-12. Triple Constraints Risk Response Strategies

Risk Response	Strategy
Leverage	Leverage strategies convert flexibility in one constraint into a resource for another constraint. Can extra time leverage increased resource availability? (Example: Using two weeks of slack lets us have access to the designer we want.) Can resources buy time? Can either buy performance? Consider rebalancing the project outcome to optimize value.
Relax	If a constraint has flexibility, then slippage in the constraint (up to the available flexibility) may significantly reduce project risk. (Example: If we rush to make the deadline, we risk quality. If two weeks late doesn't matter, we can keep quality high.) What's the impact of an extra week, an extra resource, or postponing a feature until the next upgrade?
Absorb	Directing residual and secondary risks toward the weak constraint allows your project to absorb more damage before failing. (Example: We can't afford to drop it, so we've brought in extra equipment and talent to make sure that doesn't happen.) How can you redirect impact so it mostly costs money? Does it mostly take time? Does it mostly affect a number of features?

The search for risk responses often involves asking questions, and often the answer is "no solution here." Certain questions don't apply in some situations. But you never know for sure if you don't ask.

Questions for the Weak Constraint

Project managers know that the flexibility inherent in the weak constraint is a good place to look for potential solutions. Depending on whether cost, time, or performance is your weak constraint, consider the following questions:

Cost

- Is cash a flexible resource?

- Is there an acceptable or expected degree of normal budget overrun?

- Is there someone else who can or should pay part of the bill?

- Can you borrow staff, equipment, or consumables?

- Can you borrow from other client deliverables?

- Are there resources whose costs aren't charged to your project?

- Can you exploit intangible resources (e.g., call in favors)?

Time

- Can you delay to acquire the authority to spend money in subsequent budget cycles?

- Can you use delay to improve quality or solve problems?

- Can you schedule delay to coincide with resource availability?

- Could delay lead to lower resource consumption during critical time periods?

Performance

- Can you change grade?

- Can you cut, modify, or substitute features?

- Can you cut, modify, or adjust scope?

- Will a partial delivery satisfy immediate customer needs?

- Can you fix it or upgrade it later?

Assumptions through Time and Space

That gun over there, leaning against the wall—is it loaded or unloaded?

Anyone with even a basic knowledge of gun safety knows the answer: it's loaded. Always. Even if you're sure it's empty, the assumption is always the same: it's loaded. "The gun is loaded" is indeed an assumption. Its purpose, however, is not to blind you; it's to keep you safe. If you treat the gun as if it's loaded, and it turns out to have been empty all along, there's no harm done. The other way around can be fatal.

But what if you need to *use* the gun? Maybe you no longer want to assume the gun is loaded and need to make sure there's a round in the chamber. An assumption that's useful the vast majority of the time can be counterproductive under certain circumstances.

Assumptions interact with time in several different ways. As we've seen, *circumstances* change over time. Apollo 13's mission to the moon was going well until a sudden explosion, and then the nature of the project changed instantaneously.

Knowledge changes over time. At the beginning of a project, more assumptions must be made because many of the facts aren't yet in. As you study, plan, and develop the project, assumptions freeze into facts or falsehoods.

The *environment* changes over time. We're told a foolish person builds his house on shifting sand, but modern life too often undulates like a Dalí pocket watch. Competition, technology, senior management—none of them tend to stay put very long.

The *gap* changes over time. The gap, you'll remember, predates the project—it's the difference between where one is and where one wants to be. If the reason for the project morphs, it's unavoidable that the project needs to morph with it or risk irrelevance or worse.

Known and Unknown Assumptions

"The gun is loaded" is an example of a known known assumption. We know what we're doing and why. Most risk responses are in the form of known unknown assumptions: we rent the tent, hire the paramedic, and set a rain date, acting in each case *as if* we knew the risk would occur. These types of assumptions can be healthy.

Unknown known assumptions are the product of cognitive bias. They live in our blind spots, and we must continually challenge ourselves to look through the fog our minds make for us.

And then there are unknown unknowns, where there is an absence even of assumption. In the vast universe of unknown unknowns, the things we don't even know that we don't know, there's one thing they all have in common: they would surprise us. As Monty Python so aptly reminds us: "No one expects the Spanish Inquisition!" Neither do we expect economic collapse in the midst of rapid growth, the outbreak of war in the midst of peace, or indeed any phenomenon that appears to be sailing against the zeitgeist.

To awaken your awareness of assumptions of the unknown unknowns, use negative brainstorming. These are some comparatively happy questions:

- What are some possible problems that can't happen during this project?

- What resources can we absolutely count on having, no matter what?

- What things should we not worry about at all?

- What new developments in our field cannot possibly threaten our core business value or revenue stream?

Risk and the Creative Project Manager

A creative project manager has a leg up in the quest to become a great risk manager. Even risk managers who focus on quantitative (statistical) risk know that it takes substantial insight and cleverness to make the best out of an unavoidably uncertain world.

Project risk managers have it tougher, as we've seen. The absence of certain knowledge and the role of the unknown demands a high level of thinking that is simultaneously creative and structured. The structure of the process helps you go about risk management methodically, but it's your creativity that helps find the powerful solutions.

7

Project: Intelligence

In solving a problem of this sort, the grand thing is to be able to
reason backward. That is a very useful accomplishment, and a
very easy one, but people do not practice it much. In the everyday
affairs of life it is more useful to reason forward, and so the other
comes to be neglected. There are fifty who can reason synthetically
for one who can reason analytically.
—Sherlock Holmes, in Sir Arthur Conan Doyle's
"A Study in Scarlet," 1887

THE ENVIRONMENT IN which your project operates can be almost infinitely
complex. Much of it is hidden, and even more of it is beyond your control. That predicament gives rise to an all-too-common tendency to prefer
the certain over the uncertain, the controllable over the uncontrollable.
It's uncomfortable to look into the abyss, but you have to. To make effective decisions, you need good intelligence. It's part of the due diligence of
everyday life. That's especially true for a project manager. If you don't
know what's going on, you and your project are at significant risk.

Harold Adrian Russell Philby (see Figure 7-1) was nicknamed "Kim"
by his British father after the character in Rudyard Kipling's novel of the
same name, but Kim Philby turned out not to be quite the very model of
a modern British gentleman. Instead, Kim Philby became one of the most
devastatingly successful spies in history. A double agent for the Soviet
NKVD and KGB, Philby penetrated to the highest levels of British and
American intelligence, successfully skipping town before he could be
captured.

СОВЕТСКИЙ РАЗВЕДЧИК

КИМ ФИЛБИ
1912—1988

5 к ПОЧТА СССР 1990

Figure 7-1. Kim Philby, Soviet mole in British intelligence, one of the most successful intelligence operatives of all time. This is part of a six-stamp "Great Spies of the Soviet Union" philatelic series issued in 1990.

The reflexes of a professional spy can be quite useful for a creative project manager. Spies pay attention to the environment, looking for clues and insights that provide the big picture of what's going on. Spies cultivate sources, do research, piece together clues, and manage projects. While the project management professional doesn't normally carry a Walther PPK pistol or order on-the-job martinis (shaken, not stirred), there's still an essential intelligence function that's part of any informed decision-making process. In PMBOK terms, it's the same thing as stakeholder management and monitoring environmental factors. It's just more creative (not to mention cooler) to think of it as spying.

Be assured we're not advising you to do anything unethical, much less join the KGB (or its modern equivalent). In fact, the business of intelligence can easily be described by the project management processes of stakeholder analysis and monitoring environmental factors. In stakeholder analysis, we have to figure out who the players are and what they want. In monitoring environmental factors, we have to track politics, finances, competitive activities, and changes in the marketplace. Those activities comprise an awful lot of what the U.S. Central Intelligence Agency (CIA) does—although that agency does it with more resources.

The Process of Intelligence

The best time to think through the consequences of your actions is up front. That's why taking the time to be clear about your organization's, your team's, and your own ethical boundaries is critical. Establish clear, bright lines in advance. Good guidelines are phrased in the negative ("thou shalt not") rather than the positive ("thou shalt"), because the former allows more creative freedom. In the first case, if it's not forbidden, it belongs in the realm of the possible. If, on the other hand, it's compulsory, by implication everything else is forbidden.

In order to establish guidelines, you are going to need to gather intelligence. The formal intelligence process has four phases:

1. **Collection.** Gathering the raw material of intelligence
2. **Analysis.** Extracting good information and drawing meaningful conclusions
3. **Packaging.** Organizing and preparing the information for the needs of the audience
4. **Dissemination.** Delivering and distributing information with those who have an appropriate need to know.

Let's look at each of these items in more detail.

Collection

Information isn't intelligence; it's the raw material of intelligence. You have to have information before you can analyze it. Some information is easily available, and it's wasteful not to take advantage of it. Some intelligence is available but not made public. You may pick up tidbits of information in casual conversation or notice patterns or omissions that reveal something important to your project. Often, this happens without volition on your part, although you may choose to explore the issue more actively.

Other intelligence is not made public at all, and people don't want you to have it. That doesn't automatically make the practice unethical, however. Some businesses, for example, send secret shoppers to competing retail stores to survey the competition's customers without the competition becoming aware of it.

The Types of Intelligence

Spies (and project managers) can gather five different types of information:

1. **Open source intelligence** (OSINT) gathers publicly available, well-known sources of information to analyze. Checking out the competition on Google, for example, is a use of open source intelligence.

2. **Human intelligence** (HUMINT) gathers information from human sources. Often, what's involved is simply asking questions or checking in with team members during the workday.

3. **Imagery intelligence** (IMINT) studies visual information. While in a military context that usually involves satellite or aerial photography, in the wider context you can analyze any sort of image. Marketers review the ads and brochures of competitors. Event managers may display photographs of all the very important persons, so the staff will know who's who.

4. **Signals intelligence** (SIGINT) studies signals, the transmission of information among people and machines. If you are being copied on an e-mail distribution list, you're receiving SIGINT. Paying attention to body language and behavior "tells" is signals intelligence, too.

5. **Technical intelligence** (TECHINT) studies scientific and technical information and equipment. You can buy someone else's product and tear it apart to see how it is made, or you can read reviews in trade publications.

Some of these categories may be more applicable to your project, but you shouldn't overlook any of them. You may end up ignoring important project risks that come from unexpected directions.

The Moscow Rules

In 1979, Tony Mendez, the chief of disguises at the CIA, smuggled six American diplomats out of Iran by disguising them as a Canadian film crew. He's famous for the Canadian caper, as it's known, but he's also known for codifying the Moscow Rules, a set of guidelines for cold war spy operations. Many of them are useful for project managers who need to gather stakeholder information:

1. **Do a "read-in."** The read-in technique involves getting a pre-briefing from people who have "been there and done that." Identify who has relevant knowledge, experience, and insight, and interview them before you go on site with the customer or intelligence target. That's a valuable strategy in almost any set of circumstances.

2. **Play "degrees of separation."** A good information collection technique involves figuring out how to connect yourself to the target. Whom do you know that knows somebody who knows the target? In the modern Facebook–LinkedIn world, it's easier than ever before to see how your network links up.

Cultivating and linking contacts is a full-time job, and perhaps it's not the strongest skill you have. That's okay. Look for people who are connectors—people with huge social networks—and connect to them.

3. **Don't build a profile on a single circumstance.** Unless you see people in a variety of situations, you can't truly assess their strengths, weaknesses, and goals. That's why it is important to be part of the social life of the office. Truly determined spies take the trouble to get to know their targets outside of work as well, but if you show up too many places, people get suspicious.

One good technique is to get them to come to you. Spies build "honey traps" to lure their targets. In the project office, that means keeping a well-stocked candy jar. It's a good investment in intelligence.

4. **Throw bones.** If there's information you need, you have to go after it. That means dealing with people who have that information, and they may want something in return, either now or (more dangerously) in

the future. The latter can turn into a blank check you really don't want to cash.

The biggest of slippery slopes in intelligence is that you have to give information in order to get it. That's not necessarily a problem; a lot of intelligence, as we've noted, is completely aboveboard. You can freely share information that's meant to be shared or that's openly available to anyone who cares to ask.

Information that can't be shared openly may still be able to be shared confidentially, depending on how closely held or how restricted the information happens to be.

If you're being pressed for information and there's a risk in sharing it, you've got a dilemma. The traditional strategy is that of the slow leak. If you slow down the transfer of information, a lot of it will eventually become publicly known or moot.

If you can't share information at all, pleading ignorance may work better than pleading need-to-know.

5. **Let them talk.** Listening well is a very powerful interrogation technique, because there's not a lot of listening going on in the world. People enjoy hearing the sound of their own voices, people love having their expertise and stories appreciated, and people love to show they know more about your subject than you do.

It would be a shame to deprive people of such pleasures.

Listen between the lines. What people say is important, whether it's true or false. How people lie and what they lie about tells you something true about them, if you pay attention. Body language "tells"; the attitudes of other people in the room, the topics chosen—they're all important.

Analysis

Information can be true or false, accurate or inaccurate, objective or biased, relevant or irrelevant, useful or not useful, or predictive or not predictive—and anywhere in between.

Turning raw intelligence into meaning takes analysis. Start with a question. Try this one to start:

What do you know now that you wish you had known earlier?

There is an insight born of outcome. Looking backward, it's often easy to identify the key pieces of information that would have unlocked the answer you were seeking at the time. With Sewell Avery at Montgomery Ward or Lee Iacocca at Ford, the right decisions are obvious in retrospect. But that doesn't help us when we're on the wrong end of the telescope. That's why when we have to make a decision, it's best to look around for insights as much as possible beforehand. A creative project manager probes not only the project but also the environment in which the project takes place.

Engage Enterprise *Sensors, Mr. Spock!*

The "enterprise environmental factors," as the *PMBOK Guide* calls them, cover a wide potential range: the financial condition of the organization; its competitive position; its mission, vision, and values; the choices and goals of top management; government regulation and oversight; policies and procedures; and many other aspects of organizational life.

If you've been in your organization for a while, you probably have a good understanding of the environment in which you operate, but beware of assumptions and habitual patterns of thought. Every once in a while, it's a good idea to reassess the borders of your environmental box to see if any of the constraints have changed. Sometimes they become more flexible, sometimes less so. Sometimes they vanish altogether. Sometimes new ones seem to materialize out of thin air.

In the same way that your eyes flick from mirrors to road and back again when you drive your car, you need to monitor the environment around you, with particular emphasis on the stability of the environmental assumptions. Are they accurate? Have they changed?

For Avery, convinced that the Great Depression, Part Deux, was just around the corner, the question needed to have been which signs to monitor. For Lee Iacocca, convinced that safety was at best a satisfier, not a motivator, the question should have been where to look for potential catastrophe. To find which question you should be asking, look for where threat, uncertainty, and assumptions tend to gather. That's why we recommend that you do not limit yourself to a single technique but rather apply different tools to gain new perspectives on the core problems. We can use familiar management tools, such as the fishbone diagram and the SWOT analysis, as we'll see in the following pages. Framed with the proper questions, these tools will enable you to perform a straightforward and valuable environmental analysis.

Fishbone Diagram Analysis

The fishbone diagram involves brainstorming the contributions different factors make to a common cause or problem.

This tool was developed in the 1960s by Japanese quality management innovator Kaoru Ishikawa, who called it the "cause-and-effect diagram." It's one of the seven basic tools of classical quality management. Because the drawn figure looks somewhat like the skeleton of a flounder, it's been known as the fishbone diagram ever since.

In a typical fishbone exercise (see Figure 7-2), you write a statement of an effect (e.g., a problem, an opportunity, or a goal) in a box. To the left of the box you draw a straight line, and from the straight line you draw angled lines so that the final figure resembles the backbone and spine of a fish. Each angled line represents an area that might be part of the cause.

In manufacturing, the "Four Ms"—machines (equipment and technology), methods (processes and skills), materials (raw materials and consumables), and manpower (brains and bodies)—summarize the main contributors to most effects. In the service industry, the "Eight Ps" (people, process, policies, procedures, price, promotion, place, and product) or the "Four Ss" (surroundings, suppliers, systems, and skills) are more common. Use categories that describe the big factors in your environment; alliteration is optional.

We'll follow alliteration tradition in our look at environmental factors, by using the "Four Cs": culture, corporation, community, and competition:

1. **Culture.** One of the most insightful definitions of organizational culture comes from the work of Professor Edgar Schein of MIT's Sloan School of Management. Organizational culture, Schein says, is a "pattern of shared basic assumptions that the group learned as it solved its problems of external adaptation and internal integration, that has worked well enough

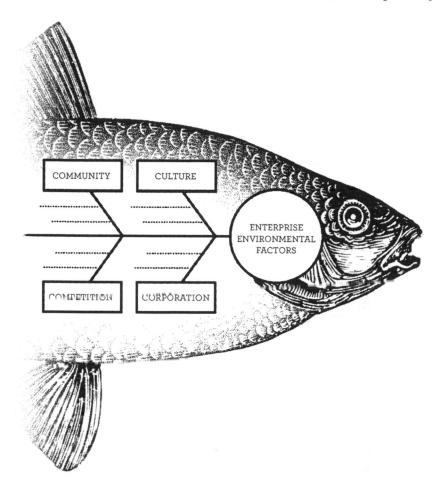

Figure 7-2. In performing a fishbone exercise, try to identify specific environmental factors in each of the categories along the spines. Break down factors to look for root causes and potential impact on your project.

to be considered valid, and therefore, to be taught to new members as the correct way you perceive, think, and feel in relation to those problems."

Organizational culture expresses itself in dress, décor, and decorum, in the creeds and credos that line the corridors, in the checks and balances that govern decisions, and in who speaks to whom and in what manner.

While many aspects of corporate culture express themselves through the agency of people, understanding the facts of culture is part of the overall environment. What are the expressed values of the organization? Does the organization actually practice those values when things get rough? If there are differences between official values and actual values, what are they? How are project constraints and pressures affected by corporate culture in both positive and negative ways? Are those expressed values expressed in everyday circumstances?

2. **Corporation.** Whether you're organized as a corporation, non-profit, government agency, or a start-up in your parents' garage, there's still a business environment around you. The environment provides both resources and constraints. What are they? What business are you in? What is your current financial condition, both as an organization and as a division or group? What resources are available, and what other organizational needs will require access to those same resources? Is your work in the mainstream of organizational efforts, or is it on the periphery? Does it challenge business units already in existence? Where is power located and concentrated?

3. **Community.** The corporation lives inside a wider community. The community spans such things as physical space (e.g., headquarters, regional offices, local branches, cities, states, and nations), business space (e.g., the real estate business or telecommunications), professional space (e.g., industry organizations, PMI, or the American Society of Training and Development), and communal space (e.g., political parties, and civic, charitable, and religious groups). Your sector and your individual organization may be known to the public in a stereotypical way (e.g., used cars or the nuclear power industry).

What are the various communities that surround the project space? Which ones affect project strategy, communications, or constraints? What assumptions exist in the various communities that may interact with the project?

4. **Competition.** Whether or not there's competition in your organizational environment may depend on your perspective. Even the government competes with other governments in some areas. Sometimes you're on good terms with your competition, other times less so. There are certain norms for competition, and certain behavior is considered off-limits. Who sets the standards? How do they affect your project?

The SWOT Analysis

Assessment of the strengths, weaknesses, opportunities, and threats (SWOT) in any business environment has also existed as a formal management technique since the 1960s. Its approach to a problem is very much in tune with an intelligence agency's. To perform a SWOT analysis (see Table 7-1), the team begins with a defined, desired end state or objective. Then, the team develops four lists, one for each area:

1. **Strengths.** These are internal characteristics of the person or the company that support achieving the objective.
2. **Weaknesses.** These are internal characteristics of the person or the company that hamper achieving the objective.
3. **Opportunities.** These are external conditions that support achieving the objective.
4. **Threats.** These are external conditions that hamper achieving the objective.

Table 7-1. Environmental SWOT analysis focuses on internal and external circumstances and conditions that affect the project in positive and negative ways

Strengths	Weaknesses
Opportunities	Threats

To improve your SWOT position, several analytical strategies are of use:

- **Building** improves strengths and opportunities.

- **Undermining** weakens the potential impact of weaknesses and threats.

- **Matching** links strengths to opportunities to identify productive avenues for competitive advantage.

- **Converting** flips or leverages threats or weaknesses into potential strengths and opportunities.

Analyze First, Research Second Technique

While analysis comes second in our list of processes, sometimes you need to analyze first, and gather the information second.

In our discussion of Patton at the Battle of the Bulge in Chapter 2, we commented on the failure of Allied High Command intelligence to see the planned German buildup. Let's look at the problem in a little more detail.

The brilliant cryptographers at Britain's Bletchley Park (code-named Station X) had cracked the top-secret German Enigma cipher in one of the most important coups of World War II. (Eisenhower himself said it was "decisive" to victory.) This vital secret (known by the code name Ultra) was so closely held that it wasn't until 1974 that the United States and Great Britain finally admitted the truth.

All kinds of careful double-blinds were put in place to keep the Germans from knowing their ciphers had been broken, meaning that some German operations that could have been foiled were instead allowed to succeed.

One of the functions of creativity is to sensitize you to important information about risks and opportunities, but the sheer volume of information, most of it devoid of real meaning, dulls your senses after a time. It takes a reason for people to look for trouble in unexpected places, and without a stimulus from Ultra, there was no reason for Allied High Command intelligence to focus on the Ardennes Forest.

Patton, a creative project manager, did look. He was stimulated by history, by his distrust of the perceptions of others, and by his own inner conviction that if he were the Germans, he'd be getting ready to throw a counterpunch.

Packaging

As you accumulate intelligence, you have to interpret, organize, and determine how best to display it. What conclusions should be drawn from the information, and what is the justification for those conclusions? What's the best way to present, organize, and share the information you have uncovered?

If you were told in early 2002 that the Pentagon had amassed a highly classified database of 946 Iraqi locations that could possibly manufacture or stockpile weapons of mass destruction (WMD)—the Iraq Master Site List (IMSL)—what would you assume? It's not unreasonable to conclude that a list that was so long served as conclusive evidence that the Iraqis were hiding at least *some* WMDs.

That turned out not to be the case.

As Operation Iraqi Freedom project planning progressed, the question of Iraqi WMDs became quite serious. If such weapons were used against attacking U.S. troops, the effects could be devastating. Project manager General James "Spider" Marks, a senior intelligence officer, needed details so that his forces could find, neutralize, and secure these sites. In late 2002 he met with Defense Intelligence Agency (DIA) officials to find out what information existed.

What were the 946 sites? They were where the Iraqis had the potential to make or store WMD materials. What did we know about the sites? Satellite photos and other technical intelligence. Were they prioritized? Yes, but not by likelihood of containing WMD materials nor by proximity to planned U.S. invasion routes, but by *suitability*.

By the time the meeting ended, Marks realized he could not be confident that even a single one of those sites contained WMDs. The culture overrelied on technical intelligence and failed to focus strongly enough on the human side. The simple fact that the database contained a large number of entries led to a cognitive bias, one epitomized by the old saying: "With this much horse manure, there's *got* to be a pony in here somewhere!"

Packaging involves framing the intelligence in a way that leads to good decisions. The oft-maligned political term *spin* has its proper uses as well. On the first day of the Cuban Missile Crisis, CIA photo intelligence director Arthur Lundahl brought the U-2 spy-plane photographs to Attorney General Robert Kennedy, who was in the middle of the effort to desegregate the University of Mississippi. Kennedy looked at the missile range diagrams, and said, "Will those [deleted] things reach Oxford, Mississippi?"

For the rest of the crisis, as a tension reliever and running joke, Lundahl added "Oxford, Mississippi" as a major city to the maps on the briefing boards.

Sometimes, the timing of information matters. There are some people to whom you don't want to bring bad news until after they've had a second cup of coffee. There's an art to deciding which news to deliver on Fridays and which on Mondays.

Visual presentation matters. Edward Tufte, noted authority on the visual presentation of information, famously argued that the *Challenger* space shuttle disaster happened at least in part because engineers failed to present the data in the right graphical form. Others argue with Tufte's analysis, but his basic point that how you present information influences how others receive it is undeniably true.

Disseminating

Who gets what part of the information you collected? Sometimes the information will be private, and you'll only be collecting it for yourself. Other times it will be necessary to share it with your whole team. You might need to provide a written report to your higher-ups, and sometimes you might need to avoid leaving a permanent hard copy, depending on what's contained within the intelligence.

Official Distribution

Regular reports, briefings, and staff meetings are official in nature. The people who receive them are prescribed by organizational policy and operational need. The information in them needs to be accurate, and it's often preserved.

Whenever possible, automate the production of routine information, and take time to format it for clarity. Presenting information graphically gets more attention than presenting the same information in words.

Special Audience Needs

In addition to official information, customers for your intelligence collection may have special issues. Pay attention to what questions they ask so you can be ready with the answer in the future. The questions themselves, as a bonus, provide insight into the mind of the questioner.

Some special needs audiences qualify because they're hostile or dismissive of information in certain areas. Perhaps they need to be won over or simply mollified. Sometimes they're active in their opposition, and you need to come prepared for argument.

Need to Know

Restricting information, however necessary or appropriate it might be, runs the risk of leaking. Don't assume you have a Kim Philby on your staff (though remember the spy adage "once is an accident, twice is a coincidence, three times is enemy action"), but keep in mind that some people talk too much. It's surprisingly easy for even random bits of information to give away far too much—or, to use the classical formulation, "loose lips sink ships."

Eyes Only

There are a number of legitimate reasons why some information needs to be restricted, but as the tabloid headline screams: "Inquiring Minds Want to Know." You can't really be sure anything is a secret unless you're sure no one else knows about it. Some intelligence is best kept completely to yourself.

The Bias of Belief

When we compared George Patton's Battle of the Bulge intelligence to that of the Supreme Allied Headquarters staff, the headquarters staff didn't look so good. The difference, of course, was less in the execution of the intelligence strategy than in the formulation of the original questions. It's important to plan for an open-ended scan of the environment to see what you can see, but focusing your major assets on the identified objective and most critical points is generally good strategy.

For a project manager, the purpose of intelligence is to make sure your understanding of the environment is as good as possible. Clarity of vision is essential to creative project management. If you don't see what's going on, no amount of creativity will help you deal with it.

That's why project managers need to be good spies.

8

It Takes a Village to Wreck a Project

Normal people . . . believe that if it ain't broke, don't fix it.
Engineers believe that if it ain't broke, it doesn't have
enough features yet.
—Scott Adams, cartoonist, creator of *Dilbert*

WHEN YOU HAVE to manage a project, you want to treat people with respect, fairness, and integrity. At the same time, there's a job that needs to
be done, and as project manager, you've been given the power to ensure
that it gets done. A discussion of people and power runs the risk of sounding manipulative and Machiavellian, and that's probably unavoidable. As
was said in another context, "That's why they call it show *business*, not
show *friends*."

Unmanaged, the people in your project environment will wreak
havoc on your objectives. If they are managed well, the situation tends to
look very different indeed. Balancing power, people skills, and integrity
requires a high level of creative project management thinking. Let's start
with power.

Power for Project Managers

Power, physicists tell us, is the energy that accomplishes some amount of
work in a certain amount of time. The corollary of no power is, all too
often, no work. The *PMBOK Guide* tells us that a project charter should
set forth the authority and the responsibility of the project manager, and

it should emphasize that the project manager must be provided the authority necessary to get the job done.

Authority is all well and good, but it's not the final word on power. Office politics authority Marilyn Moats Kennedy observed, "Want to know if you're a leader? Look back and see if anyone's following." That's as neat an operational definition as we've heard. While other people can give you authority, they can also take it away. Only you can give yourself the power that really matters.

Four Managerial Challenges

Tensions between authority and power are hardly new to the project manager—or indeed to managers in general. The bitterest pain, wrote Herodotus in the fifth century BCE, was to have much knowledge and little power. Unfortunately, nothing much has changed on that score in the last 2,500 years.

How much power you need varies by the job. Authority might be very high in absolute terms, but if you're fighting a Godzilla-sized crisis, it may be grossly insufficient to the problem at hand. Your formal authority, which is supposed to be written in the project charter, is important, and it's worth trying to negotiate for what you think you really need. But it's still not really enough. Inevitably, there are mismatches between authority and responsibility, which can lead to four distinct problems, as shown in Figure 8-1.

There's a common saying among project managers that a project goes through predictable life cycle phases: enthusiasm, disillusionment, panic, search for the guilty, punishment of the innocent, praise and promotions for nonparticipants—and much later, if at all, definition of the requirements.

When things go well, there's no shortage of people willing to share the credit. When things go wrong, the project manager is a prime suspect—and occasionally a scapegoat. To know how to manage yourself, you have to know how you're being perceived. Let's examine each type of mismatch.

1. **Martyr.** You risk being viewed as a project management martyr when you've got a very big job with problematic odds of a good outcome.

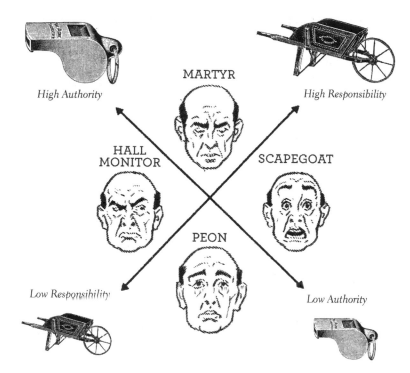

Figure 8-1. The mismatch of authority and responsibility can create four distinct management challenges for any project manager.

When "failure is not an option" and at the same time it's a very likely possibility, the project manager is at great risk of being elected the captain who needs to go down with the ship.

Project managers with high integrity are particularly vulnerable, because they don't like yielding in the face of challenges, and sometimes they continue past the point of common sense and self-preservation. Or, as comic book sage Stan Lee wrote, "With great power comes great responsibility."

2. **Hall monitor.** Petty power, research shows, is more often abused than substantial power. If a project manager doesn't have the power to make important decisions, the tendency is to oversee the small stuff with an iron hand. This comes from a feeling of being out of control overall. Hall monitors are usually reacting against stress somewhere else. If you're

experiencing substantial stress, double-check to make sure you're not taking it out on the wrong people.

3. **Scapegoat.** When the responsibility is outsized compared to the authority, guess who's going to take the fall? Make sure you know when you're in that role. It may not be personal or deliberate, merely circumstantial. Follow the old rule that if you can't figure out who's the sucker in the poker game, it must be you.

What are the internal consequences if the project fails? Will political enemies make hay of it? Will failure result in layoffs or reorganizations? If the internal effects are negative enough, sometimes people start looking for blood. This search will probably lead them to the project manager. If you think you're potentially vulnerable to be cast in a scapegoat role, you need to start maneuvering well in advance.

4. **Peon.** "I must be a mushroom," goes the old saying. "They keep me in the dark, they feed me manure, and then they can me." There are problems you might be able to solve and needs you could easily meet, but they fall outside the areas of your responsibility and your authority, regardless of the degree of Herodotean knowledge you bring to the table. Somehow the right projects for your skill set tend to elude you.

Almost everyone starts as a peon, and that's as it should be. However, if you stay a peon longer than your contemporaries, you might want to figure out why. It's very common for a person of significant technical skill to be less effective on the people side, and the latter is the ticket to management.

You're not destined to end up in any of the quadrants discussed above, but some people do. It's obviously vital to recognize when you're cast in one of these roles, but it's good to know when other people are stuck in them, too. One very good thing you can do as a creative project manager is help others out of these traps. Everyone benefits.

Six Sources of Power

One way to address a mismatch between authority and responsibility as a project manager is to attain more power. The source of organizational power we know best is the official power that comes with our role, but sadly, that is often insufficient. In most organizations, there's a vice president without the authority to sneeze and at least one clerk with the power of life and death. Official power isn't necessarily the same as real power. People often represent themselves as having significant power, and why shouldn't they? However, you need to know whether you're dealing with someone who has the power to make a decision or you're working with a go-between.

There are six different sources of organizational power, shown in Figure 8-2. One way to use the model is to identify your strengths and weaknesses and then grow your power. Another way is to use it to analyze the power of others, as a tool to help you manage them better.

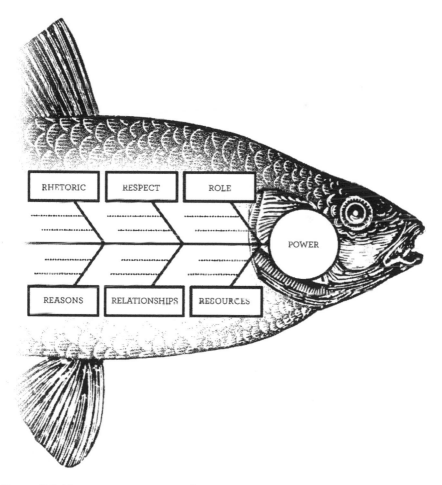

Figure 8-2. You can map your organizational power in six categories using this fishbone diagram.

What you can't afford to do is ignore power. As a project manager, you tend to have too little in the first place. It's your job to pick up the rest.

The six sources of power are the following:

1. Role
2. Respect
3. Rhetoric
4. Resources
5. Relationships
6. Reasons

We'll be using the fishbone diagram technique (explained in Chapter 7) to examine these in more detail.

Role

Your role power comes with a title and rank. It includes both long-term components (e.g., the job title) and short-term ones (e.g., the project assignment), and sometimes it includes secondary roles (e.g., being seconded to the project management organization part time to advise on IT issues). Role power is always delegated. It belongs to the organization, not to you. Whatsoever the organization giveth, it also can taketh away. Make sure that you know the extent to which people will listen to you because of your title and position.

Respect

By contrast, power from respect belongs primarily to you. The organization cannot command respect on your behalf, nor can it easily deprive you of respect once it has been earned. There are many subspecies of respect power. You can be respected for your character, for your integrity, for your competence, for your track record, for your technical or subject-matter expertise, for your wisdom, for your judgment, and indeed for many other qualities. Remember, though, that respect is an earned credit that can be spent. History is littered with famous people who stored up great respect and then lost it all.

You can also be respected for negative reasons, the same way that people respect a rattlesnake for the danger it represents. This respect slides into the fear side of the spectrum, although even fear has its legitimate uses. However, fear also makes people want to deceive you, so it's a power best used with extreme care and moderation.

Rhetoric

The art form known as oratory—using words to persuade—is a fundamental source of power. From running an effective meeting to putting together a good PowerPoint show, from negotiating a contract to persuading a colleague to cooperate with the project objective, skill in communication is essential to project management effectiveness. Later in this chapter, we'll explore some communication strategies that a creative project manager can use to strengthen himself or herself in this vital dimension.

Negotiation skills are also part of rhetoric that calls for creativity—the art of finding win/win solutions. It's much easier to persuade people when they're going to benefit. They don't begrudge you your victories; they begrudge their defeats.

Resources

Control of resources is an oft-overlooked source of power, and most people wield it poorly, either by using the opportunity to punish their enemies (which often backfires), or by failing to appreciate the political dimension of resource appropriation (which can waste legitimate opportunity). Giving out certain resources provides organizational and personal benefits at the same time. Advanced training is a resource for the organization, but it's simultaneously a benefit to the trainee who receives it. If there's no objective reason why the trainee must be a specific person, you can certainly take into account such factors as cooperativeness and team spirit in deciding who gets the prize.

Sometimes you have to give out resources nobody wants, and that's a delicate matter, too. People tend to have an exaggerated sense of how many times they've drawn the short straw, so it's incumbent upon you to keep track and make sure the allocation is appropriate. (This doesn't imply the allocation should always be equal.)

Managing resources often means reducing resources, and taking resources away always creates conflict. How you cut resources—a 10 percent across-the-board slash or a more detailed and thoughtful pruning of projects and initiatives — has huge organizational implications. Without substantial respect power to support you, cutting resources is a very bad situation in which to find oneself.

Relationships

Who you know always matters, and the smart project manager cultivates a wide network of contacts. By their very nature, projects tend to slice laterally through the organization, and movement from stovepipe to stovepipe is inherently more sluggish than movement up and down in the same column of the organization chart.

Relationship management also ties in with resources, and it's a powerful tool for smoothing the conflicts that inevitably result from resource allocation. Leveraging resources for power and leveraging relationships for power have a lot in common. Both improve in effectiveness when you adopt an abundance mentality, the operating assumption being that there are enough resources and success opportunities to go around.

Be generous with the favors and support you provide to other people. The positive effect you'll get in terms of relationship building is often disproportionate to the cost to you. Don't look at favors on a quid pro quo basis. Honorable people look for the opportunity to repay kindness with kindness, and even the less honorable may be better disposed toward you.

Reasons

At the heart of power is the question of why you want it in the first place, and that reason can be a force multiplier — or, in some cases, a weakener. If power is energy used to accomplish work, then the question becomes, what sort of work? If the purpose of your power is solely self-protection and self-aggrandizement, other people will see it quickly enough, and you'll lose power in the respect department.

The primary reason, the value of the project itself, isn't always under your control. If the team thinks the project is a bad idea, their commitment to success will necessarily be compromised.

Secondary reasons matter too, and some of these are completely under your control. If it's important to you to help people learn new skills or to make the team function smoothly, you'll likely get better cooperation. Ethics and integrity count in this category as well.

Alignment is part of reason power. When your values and goals are aligned with the organization, power tends to flow your way. If your mission conflicts with broader organizational currents, fairly or unfairly, expect your power center to erode.

The Ethics of Power

Power is, by itself, ethically neutral. Ethical questions arise when you consider how to get it, how to use it, and what you're hoping to achieve with it. As we recommended in discussion of the ethics of intelligence gathering in Chapter 7, the best move is to establish clear ethical standards before you go into the project, lest you find yourself drifting over a fuzzy line you weren't even aware was there.

In establishing your own clear ethical boundaries in situations that may be fuzzy or subjective, orient yourself by asking two questions:

1. Am I confident no one will suffer a negative outcome from my behavior?
2. Would I be pleased if other people used the same tactic to achieve their goals?

If the answer to these two questions is unambiguously positive, you're entitled to a presumption the behavior is clearly ethical. If the answer to either isn't a clear yes, then it's time to assess the ethical dimensions of your choice very carefully. That doesn't always mean you shouldn't take the action; it only means you need to think before you act and be sure you are using your power in an ethically responsible way.

Power in Practice: Eisenhower and Patton

You don't have to be a master of all forms of power to be successful. If you understand the components of your power, you can surround yourself with a team that complements your strengths and weaknesses. If you could do it all by yourself, then it wouldn't be a very big project. Project leadership means leveraging your power through the work of others.

In very different ways, Dwight D. Eisenhower and George S. Patton demonstrate the use of power in leadership.

Eisenhower

Eisenhower's challenge in leading the wartime alliance in the West was to wrestle a fractious, politically charged alliance into an effective fighting machine under severe time and resource constraints. Yes, he made mistakes and sometimes showed poor judgment, but he was handed an impossible job, and no one could have done it perfectly.

Eisenhower needed power to do his job. Let's see just how he stacked up on the six sources of power as he embarked on this fateful project.

1. **Role.** It's clear that you can't just pin five stars on someone's shoulder and make an invasion happen. The power of the role, though formidable, doesn't automatically provide the skills and operational art to do the work. Indeed, though Eisenhower's role power was very high in absolute terms, in his orbit plenty of other people were even more powerful than he.

2. **Respect.** He was certainly respected—brilliant, hard working, focused, a leader. Respect is somewhat relative in this instance, though; wartime produced a number of great leaders, and in Eisenhower's world, being highly respected was taken for granted.

3. **Rhetoric.** He was not known as a gifted writer or speaker. He was clearly persuasive with individuals and small groups, but he was largely unproven in addressing or inspiring larger audiences.

4. **Resources.** Eisenhower's role included the ability to command huge resources in support of his objective. That's not quite the same thing as saying he had a blank check; there were real limits as well. A shortage of gasoline forced Eisenhower to make a critical (and often criticized) choice to supply Montgomery's 21st Army Group instead of Patton's Third Army.

5. **Relationships.** Eisenhower's relationship management skills were clearly extraordinary. In spite of the five stars on his shoulder, Eisenhower was frequently not the most powerful person in the room. Managing the political environment was a full-time job.

6. **Reason.** Although Eisenhower was known to be personally ambitious, he was also known as a man of high integrity who was in fact dedicated to the mission. By subordinating his personal goals to his cause, he made himself more effective. The way to get ahead is to know how to put the bigger picture first.

Patton

Patton was a very different kind of leader, but he had a very different kind of mission. He was supposed to take a small city—which is what an army at war essentially is—and make it move and fight. This is an immense, complex operation that requires a top-notch planning staff and detailed coordination in the face of considerable uncertainty. It requires a leadership approach that is both authoritarian and empowering. Let's take a look at Patton through the six sources of power.

1. **Role.** As a three-star general, Patton was the equivalent of a corporate division president. He had a significant operational area for which he held profit-and-loss responsibility, and his job was to make his division meet its numbers.

2. **Respect.** Patton was admired for what he did well, but he had lost dramatic amounts of respect and goodwill through his public misbehaviors, such as the infamous incident in which Patton slapped a soldier suffering from battle fatigue while reporters watched. Neither Eisenhower nor Bradley completely trusted Patton, which weakened his power significantly.

3. **Rhetoric.** Patton was a gifted—if remarkably profane—speaker and a surprisingly good historian and writer. This gave him many advantages. The ability to motivate an army is important, but also important is

the ability to turn your ideas into policies. Patton was an inevitable candidate for a very senior operational role because he'd been active in the development of the doctrines he fought with. Writing reports is an underrated strategic skill.

4. **Resources.** Patton was weak in one of his critical resources: gasoline. When the Third Army was poised to penetrate into Germany, Patton needed a generous allotment of scarce gasoline. Eisenhower, the resource owner, had to consider a number of factors, not merely Patton's needs, in making his decision. Patton's own reputation, alas, didn't help his case.

5. **Relationships.** Patton was a shouter with a terrible temper, though he was capable of extreme kindness and thoughtfulness on occasion. He was known to be trouble. He made enemies within his own ranks (his former subordinate, Omar Bradley, was not a fan), and this weakened him as well.

6. **Reason.** Patton's skill at his vital job was enough to counterbalance the trouble he caused all too often. He was rebellious, anti-authoritarian (except where his own authority was concerned), temperamental, and difficult. Through sheer talent he survived, but his ability to get resources at critical moments was hampered by his inability to work well with the larger organization.

Dwight David Eisenhower had his weaknesses, but he knew how to compensate for them by surrounding himself with talent. George Patton also had weaknesses, but he didn't compensate for them. Instead, he relied on his merit as a fighting general (which was high) to offset his flaws. That latter approach is not as good as the former.

With no disrespect to Patton's clear military genius, Eisenhower makes a better role model.

Stakes and Holders

Understanding power takes us into the wider people environment of your project: stakeholders. The power of your stakeholders can have profound effects on your project, and knowing how to manage them is one of the purposes of getting power in the first place.

Stakeholders are the people who have a stake in your project, either in the outcome or in the process. Notice that the nature of the stake can change during the project life cycle; people can become stakeholders, become different stakeholders, or become non-stakeholders. Don't assume stability.

Four Types of Stakeholders

At the first level of triage, stakeholders can be sorted into four approximate groups:

1. **Positive stakeholders,** who stand to gain through the project's outcome or process
2. **Negative stakeholders,** who stand to lose through the project's outcome or process
3. **Tangential stakeholders,** who have an unrelated or secondary interest in the project's outcome or process
4. **Conflicted stakeholders,** who have conflicting interests in more than one area of the project

Positive stakeholders may not always have goals identical to yours, but there's always alignment. You want a good product from your vendor; your vendor wants to be paid and get repeat business. These interests are not identical, but they are linked. Look for potential positive stakeholders who aren't obvious. You may be ignoring important assets who are only waiting to be asked. Others may not understand why their interests will benefit from your project's process or outcome and need to be shown.

Negative stakeholders may be in broad agreement but have a particular sticking point, or they may be opposed in principle. Sticking points can often be resolved; principles less so. If there's a personal or emotional interest involved, it's important for you to know the hot buttons. Look for areas where win/win is possible. It's important to build trusting relationships with negative stakeholders; you frequently have to do business with them.

Tangential stakeholders see an unrelated opportunity in or threat from your project. If they combine their order with yours, for example, it will qualify for a volume discount. Depending on how their needs are managed, they may turn positive or negative, or they may cease to be stakeholders altogether.

Conflicted stakeholders have interests in more than one category, but unlike tangential stakeholders, they are usually more entangled in the project environment. We believe negotiation is an absolute core competency for project managers; it is in the volatile environment of conflicted stakeholders that all your skills come to bear.

Office Politics

The roster of players in your project environment is one of the chief factors that affects how any project will play out; therefore, the people working with you on the project you're managing are stakeholders, and the office politics that goes on among them is another factor in your project. There's a very simple test to measure whether office politics is taking a toll on your environment: do a headcount, and if the number exceeds three, it is. Politics is a source of a lot of organizational stress—but politics is also ubiquitous, and you can seldom safely stay on the sidelines.

Our definition of politics is "the informal and sometimes emotion-driven process of allocating limited resources and working out goals, decisions, and actions in an environment of people with different and competing interests and personalities." You'll notice that this could almost be a blanket definition of project management. Nobody checks his or her humanity at the door when working on a project.

Some interests are self-serving, others oriented more toward teamwork and organizational goals. Don't assume self-serving interests are bad. Instead, ask yourself how you can leverage them to achieve wider goals. After all, paychecks, promotions, and bonus awards are ways to link people's financial interests to organizational goals. That's a *good* thing.

As we've noted, one part of being a creative project manager is being a creative negotiator. Negotiation is one tool to bring your team into alignment.

Managing Stakeholders

There are four stages in stakeholder management, as shown in Table 8-1.

Table 8-1. Four Stages of Managing Stakeholders

Stage	Strategy
Identify	Who is affected by the project positively, negatively, or tangentially? How much can they affect the project outcome?
Understand	What is the nature of the stakeholder interest? Is it process or product, core or peripheral? Are there personal or emotional issues involved?
Maximize	What can be done to address the needs of this stakeholder? How can the stakeholder be positioned for best advantage to the project?
Manage	What care does the stakeholder require? How often and in what way do you need to communicate? Is the stakeholder's position or interest likely to change?

Interest and Importance

If it's easy to satisfy a stakeholder, even a marginal one, it's worth doing for the goodwill, even if there's no other obvious benefit. When satisfying a stakeholder is difficult, problematic, or potentially impossible, you have to consider the risks; use the questions in Table 8-2.

Table 8-2. Stakeholder Interests and Impact

Questions	Issues
What does the stakeholder want?	Needs can be personal or professional, based on principle or narrow interests. Some needs are hinted; others explicit.
What are the consequences to the stakeholder for not getting it?	Consequences can involve material loss or psychological loss. They can be severe or minor. Some are so important the stakeholder cannot afford to lose; others can be negotiated away with ease.
What can the stakeholder do to influence the situation?	Some stakeholders have legitimate positional power; others have political influence; still others have money or other resources to offer.
How likely is conflict with this stakeholder?	Depending on what's at stake, the personality and temperament of the stakeholder, and the previous history with you or your organization, you may need to prepare for conflict as one element of your risk plan.

Stakeholders don't necessarily sit still. While some stakeholders are with you for the life of the project (or beyond), others have a narrower situational interest. The accounting department needs billing statements on time. The vice president had better have a demonstration to show at the quarterly executive retreat. The legal department needs to make sure you're keeping a complete backup set of your e-mails. The overall success or failure of the project, in terms of their interests, is at best secondary. People will pass in and out of your stakeholder environment throughout the life of the project.

Situations change, and stakeholder needs and positions often change with them. Someone who preferred a different approach might decide to get on board when it's clear the train is leaving the station. New evidence may convince someone to change a previously solid position. Sometimes, it comes down to the project manager's way or the highway. If the need for altering your tactics or approach comes up, try not to hold a grudge for behavior that is no longer motivated, but be aware that most people can't manage this. Even if you succeed in putting the past behind, the other person may have a slow-burning fuse.

Stakeholder Communications Management

Developing a communications plan is a practice recommended by the *PMBOK Guide*, but it focuses primarily on the mechanics of project reporting. Stakeholders need to know whether milestones are being met, whether the project is moving in accordance with its baseline, and whether there are any current problems or issues of interest. Political communication—the kind you need for stakeholder management—is a bit more sophisticated. When you are in a position of power over a project, you are going to have to communicate frequently with your team members and many other stakeholders as it develops. Let's take a macro look at communication, since it's such an important part of being in charge.

Communications

Why do we communicate? We have thoughts, desires, dreams, and ideas in our minds, but to make anything happen, that information has to reach someone else's mind. That process is communication.

Three Goals of Communication

There are only three reasons to communicate: (1) you want someone to do something; (2) you want someone to know something; or (3) you want someone to feel something—or some combination of the three. One of the quickest ways to improve the quality of your communication is to be clear in your mind about what outcome you are seeking, and work backward from there. Table 8-3 lists strategic questions for each goal to help you get clarity.

Table 8-3. Three Goals of Communication

Goal	Techniques
Do	What is the desired action? When does it need to take place? What resources or tools are needed, and how can they be obtained? What is the value or importance of the action? Are there risks and costs involved? Why should the person perform the action you desire? What's in it for them? How will you verify that the desired action has been taken?
Know	What is the information you want the other person to know? Is it clearly presented? What medium will communicate the information best (writing, drawing, talking, spreadsheet, etc.)? What proof or evidence can you offer that the knowledge is correct? What is the value of the knowledge? How will the receiver use the knowledge? Will the receiver resist the knowledge? How will you verify that the knowledge has been successfully communicated?
Feel	What emotion or attitude do you want the receiver to adopt? What emotion or attitude does the receiver currently have? What is the reason for the receiver's current emotion? Will an emotional appeal or a factual appeal have the greatest impact? What media or approach is likely to work best? How will you verify that the receiver now has the desired emotion or attitude?

Three Steps of Communication

The classic model of communication is known as the sender-receiver model, in which ordinary oral communication is considered in engineering terms. To communicate, you start with a thought. Next, you encode that thought into language and broadcast your message as speech. Whether consciously or not, you send additional information in the tone of your voice and your visual appearance (e.g., dress and body language).

The sound waves of your message travel through the physical environment, where they are subject to interruption and distraction—the message doesn't always get through completely and correctly. The receiver has to break down the message that is received—including tone and visual—and does so while filtering the information through preconceived knowledge, ideas, attitudes and emotions.

When you think of all the steps your message has to go through, it's not surprising how often we are misunderstood. It's a miracle that anybody ever understands anything! In planning your communication, realize that each message has to go through three stages before it can achieve your "do/know/feel" objective, as shown in Table 8-4.

Table 8-4. Three Levels of Communication

Level	Issues
Message received	The first step in any communication is to make sure that your message has been received. No one, after all, is obligated to follow a nonexistent directive.
Message under-stood	The second step in any communication is to make sure that your message has been understood. That doesn't automatically mean that the receiver agrees with the message, but it's fundamental that the receiver at least understands what it is you wish to happen.
Message resolved	The third and final step in any communication is to ensure that your message has been accepted or rejected. The ideal outcome is that acceptance equals agreement and you will achieve your communications goal. If the message is rejected, you still need to know that, so that you can plan your next steps

Managing Conflict

Conflict is the name we use whenever there's a difference between two people. Whether it's over something as simple as where to go to lunch today or as complex as the prescription for Middle East peace, conflict is woven into the fabric of our everyday lives. Conflict isn't automatically negative, although it certainly can be. It can also be an opportunity for greater understanding, a way to resolve problems, or in some trivial cases, something to be ignored or dismissed.

Conflict involves actual or perceived clashes of needs, wants, values, and interests, and it ranges in intensity from polite conversation all the way to war. Conflicts can cause varying amounts of damage, and they may be resolved well or poorly. Project management is a field where conflict is inevitable and common. Stakeholders have needs, wants, values, and interests. Resources are limited. Your goal is to manage inevitable conflict in the most effective way possible.

PMI identifies various strategies for managing conflict: smoothing, withdrawal, compromise, forcing, and confrontation (see Figure 8-3). Of these, according to PMI, confrontation (we think *negotiation* is a better word) is the strategy normally preferred by project managers. That preference is fraught with danger. In point of fact, every single one of these strategies has a time and place in which it is the best solution. Two variables should influence your decision as to which strategy to use.

First, how important is achieving your goal to you? If life and death are at stake, your goals are very important to you. If the question is where we're going to have lunch today, your goals may matter a lot less.

Second—and this is a little more subtle—how important is the *other* person's goal to *you?* If the conflict is with someone you care about, making him or her happy may be very important to you. Keeping customers, bosses, and coworkers happy is normally worth some minor concessions on your part. Other times, what the other person wants may not matter to you.

Once you've figured out how important your needs are to you, and how important *their* needs are to you (not to them), you can choose the most effective strategy. Maybe you want to smooth over the conflict, maybe you want to give in, maybe compromise is in order, maybe it's time to apply some pressure, or maybe there's a way to resolve the conflict so that everyone wins. Here's more detail on each of the strategies shown in Figure 8-3.

■ **Smoothing.** Sometimes winning isn't the issue. Let's say that the project you're managing is the assembly of a peaceful Thanksgiving dinner with the extended family. During this meal, someone brings up one of those perfectly inappropriate dinner table conversation topics—like abortion. No matter how passionate your beliefs are about this topic, this isn't the time and place for the discussion, so you avoid the conflict by changing the subject . . . and thus smoothing away the conflict before it occurs.

■ **Withdrawal.** Sometimes, as noted, the other person's needs are more important to you than your own, and you can withdraw or surrender.

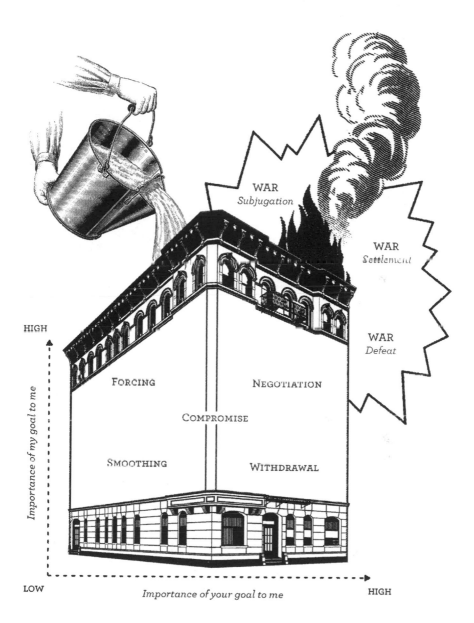

Figure 8-3. The Conflict Resolution Grid shows the range of available strategies to manage conflict.

Let's imagine we're all going out to eat. If someone in the group really hates Thai food, you might suggest that you all go somewhere else, even though Thai is your favorite cuisine. Or you may simply know you'll be outvoted anyway, so you decide to surrender gracefully.

■ **Compromise.** Or maybe someone doesn't like Thai food and you don't like sushi, so as a compromise, the group goes to an Indian restaurant. If everyone likes Indian food well enough, even if each person has a different favorite national cuisine, everyone can have a nice dinner. But if no one in the group likes Indian food, then the compromise has made the situation worse.

■ **Forcing.** You could insist that everyone agree to Thai food or you'll refuse to go to dinner. You might have a good reason for doing so; perhaps some food allergy or dietary restriction makes it impossible for you to go anywhere else.

■ **Negotiation.** The group could discuss what everyone liked to eat, and, with luck, find a choice that would delight everyone—a "win/win." This approach takes more time and effort, but potentially it yields the best answer.

Thinking Win/Win

We've talked about the creative approach to negotiation, thinking win/win. Win/win is an idea that sounds impractical, no matter how desirable it might be. How can both sides win?

Harvard negotiation experts Roger Fisher and William Ury in their seminal work *Getting to Yes* tell the story of the two sisters fighting over the last orange. They decide to settle the argument by compromise, cutting the orange down the middle and each taking half. One sister is hungry. She peels her half, eats the fruit, and throws the peel away. The other sister, however, is baking. She takes her half, peels it, throws the fruit away, and carries the peel into the kitchen to grate for her recipe.

Interests are different from positions. The position is what we're asking for. ("I want the orange," or "I want to eat Thai food.") The interest, on the other hand, is why you want it. ("I need some grated orange peel," or "Red curry is my favorite dish.") You can't negotiate positions. You get the whole orange, you don't get the orange, or you cut it in half. Interests, on the other hand, aren't necessarily reciprocal. If Sister A wants the fruit and Sister B wants the peel, they can peel the orange and each get 100 percent of what each wants. If you want to buy something from someone, you want that person's stuff more than you want to keep your money. That person wants your money more than he wants to keep all his stuff. Both win.

If the project has any substance to it, you can't do it alone. Aligning the project team, stakeholders, customers, and the organization to achieve a common goal requires a combination of Eisenhower's skills and Patton's skills. Knowing when to be diplomatic and when to be forceful is a delicate art. Patton, to his detriment, never mastered it.

You can't afford to make the same mistake.

9

Framing Change

I confess that in 1901 I said to my brother Orville that man would not
fly for fifty years. Two years later we ourselves made flights.
This demonstration of my impotence as a prophet gave me such a shock
that ever since I have distrusted myself and avoided all predictions.
—Wilbur Wright (1867–1912), in a speech to the
Aero Club of France, November 5, 1908

WHAT'S HALF OF thirteen (13)? There's more than one right answer. There's
6½, but it could also be half of the word *thirteen*: "*thir*" or "*teen*." Or it
could be the number 1 or 3, which comprise the number 13. Each of these
answers is correct when seen through a particular frame. Frames are situational; they're useful or not useful, not right or wrong.

The way you frame project change has profound implications for
how you understand it, plan for it, and cope with it. Change management
is one of the major challenges facing project managers in any field of endeavor. People change. Technology changes. Needs change. The environment changes. Change can't be controlled, and change can't be
eliminated—nor should it be.

That doesn't mean that change is always fun.

Here are three important truths about change:

1. All change creates some loss.
2. Change tends to make things worse in the short run.
3. The price of change must be paid; the payoff is not guaranteed.

Even when the change is beneficial overall, there's still some loss and at least short-term headache to contend with. The best solution is to make sure the payoff happens; however, strategies to diminish loss and reduce those short-term headaches pay dividends, too. The creative project manager overlooks no possible solutions.

Change, of course, can be positive and even exhilarating, filled with opportunity. Often, your ability to experience change in a positive way is at least as much a function of your personal attitude as it is with the actual facts of the situation.

In this chapter, we'll explore a particular technique to help you, the creative project manager, frame change constructively: to see patterns and analogies, make predictions about the future, and develop strategies to achieve your project and organizational goals.

The way we'll go about it is a technique you've seen us practice throughout this book: using patterns in the past as a guide to the future.

Manage the Past, Manage the Future

The speed and severity of change in your environment is a known stressor. Today's world is experiencing change at a rate never before experienced in human history; nevertheless, our past is still a useful resource to help us deal with our future.

The Stone Age, Bronze Age, and Iron Age each occupied thousands of years of human prehistory. The Industrial Revolution occupied only a few hundred; the Age of Steam power spanned mere decades. Electricity dominated the *fin de siècle* (i.e., the last years of the nineteenth century), and combustion engines defined the early years of the twentieth century. The Atomic Age was born in a cloud over Hiroshima in 1945, but a mere 12 years later a beeping Sputnik announced that the Space Age had arrived. The dawning of the Age of Aquarius paralleled the opening of the Information Age: ARPANET (the Advanced Research Projects Agency Network), the predecessor to today's Internet, was conceived in 1962, and by 1969 it consisted of only four nodes.

The technical revolution in all its manifestations—energy, pharmaceuticals, information technology, and medicine—just keeps on coming. Each new iteration arrives at the speed of change, nipping at the heels of its predecessor.

Projects are often the mechanism by which this kind of change takes place. Many project managers find ourselves in an environment significantly more fluid than that of even our Space Age predecessors of a few short decades ago, landing on the moon with 48 kilobytes of onboard computer processing power.

Tomorrow will bring more of the same. How can you as a project manager cope with continual environmental change?

Why, creatively, of course.

Alternate Futures, Alternate Pasts

One technique for coping with change comes from the place where history meets science fiction: the topic of "counterfactuals." A counterfactual is an extrapolation of what might have happened if some actual event in history turned out another way. Here's an example.

In 1944, a disaffected German officer named Claus von Stauffenberg planted a bomb hidden in a briefcase in Adolf Hitler's conference room at Wolfschanze (Wolf's Lair), the führer's forest retreat. Another officer, Heinz Brandt, sat down at the table, and his feet bumped the briefcase. He picked it up and placed it behind a concrete post, inadvertently saving Hitler's life.

Unlucky accident undid von Stauffenberg's plan. Risk is one source of the kind of change that can upset the best-laid Gantt charts of mice and men. Other sources of change are not necessarily triggered by accidents, but they too can be highly disruptive.

In the case of von Stauffenberg, it's interesting and instructive to ask, "What if?" What if Brandt hadn't moved the briefcase, so that the bomb went off as planned, killing the führer? Would project success (i.e., killing Hitler) have closed the project gap (i.e., ending Nazi rule in Germany)?

Our analysis of the counterfactual argues that it would not. The plan relied on several senior Wehrmacht officers leading their armies in revolt, and one of them (Field Marshal Erwin Rommel) was in the hospital recovering from very serious wounds. The plan also required a program of assassinations to take out most of the senior Nazi leadership. Failure to take out, for example, the very well-guarded Reichsführer-SS Heinrich Himmler, who had his own army, would be quite literally fatal for all concerned. As it stood, about three hundred people were tortured to death for their alleged role in the conspiracy, many hanged with barbed-wire nooses.

Rommel was offered—and he accepted—the opportunity to commit suicide instead.

For project managers, counterfactuals are a great way to analyze the effect of potential changes. You can use the technique on your own or with a small brainstorming group. To avoid groupthink, assign roles to the participants: your job is to be the competition and decide how you can best disrupt our plans, and your job is to be the financial department and make sure we spend as little as possible. Pick a change and extrapolate from it, or pick a desired target and extrapolate backward. For example, you might want to explore what might happen if a competitor were to release a similar product; so begin with that assumption and try to manage forward from that point. Or, you could imagine a situation (e.g., our profit margin has doubled) and work backward to figure out what might lead to that goal.

Planes, Change, and Automobiles

In addition to counterfactuals, you can gain insight into changes by studying the development of parallel events. How have projects similar to yours changed?

In 1914, the car of automobile racer Barney Oldfield (the "fastest man alive") could outrace aviator Lincoln Beachey's flying machine. A SWOT analysis (see Chapter 7) might conclude the airplane posed little threat to automobile and rail transportation. In 1914, that was a fair assessment.

But it doesn't stay 1914 forever.

We know how radically the capabilities of both automobiles and airplanes have changed. Their respective impacts on commerce and interrelationship have changed with each advancement in technology. They are only competitive in narrow areas of overlap; each serves special needs.

Nevertheless, as shown in Table 9-1, there are lots of parallels between cars and airplanes, and between yesterday's change and today's versions. Use the questions in the table to figure out some good analogies to inform you about your own project.

Table 9-1. 1914 Business Issues for the Automobile and Airplane Industries

Question	Potential Insights
What is your business? (State so as simply as possible.)	Both cars and airplanes, in one sense, are in the same business. They move people and things from one point to another.
How was the need met before your solution came along?	People and things have always needed to get from one point to another, and a variety of human, animal, and technological solutions have been employed through the ages. The biggest current competitor is passenger rail.
What is the origin of the products or methods you use?	Car is short for "carriage," a passenger contrivance with a source of motive power. The "horseless carriage" changes the motive power from horses to mechanical energy. The first airplane designers copied birds for their vehicles (i.e., ornithopters), until the Wright Brothers used kites and wind tunnels to learn how to create and take advantage of lift.
Does the flowchart for the process resemble any other processes?	Logistics management, systems engineering, bird migration, fluid dynamics, game theory— you can map any number of processes to these business areas.

Both the automobile and aircraft industries have gone through a series of transformations over the years, and business models have come and gone. Until the introduction of the 21-seat DC-3 in 1935, no airliner was able to operate at a profit on passengers alone; an airmail contract was essential.

Both modes of transportation have faced stiff competition. Railroads, ships, mass transit vehicles, and even bicycles each serve their own constituencies by offering advantages that neither airplanes nor automobiles can match. We could easily shift the frame of reference, however, and say that airplanes and automobiles offer advantages that the others cannot, and sometimes that other frame of reference will produce insights we cannot see directly. When we look back at the past, everything that happens seems inevitable in retrospect, but it never looks that way through the wrong historical end of the telescope.

Compare the 1914 snapshot mentioned previously with 2009 (see Table 9-2).

Table 9-2. 2009 Business Issues for the Automobile and Airplane Industries

Question	Potential Insights
What is your business? (State so as simply as possible.)	The fundamentals are unchanged. As the price has dropped and infrastructure has improved, more people and things move from one point to another for more different reasons than ever before. This has brought many more players into the market, and it has saturated many product categories.
How was the need met before your solution came along?	In general, it was met less well and less expensively. Nevertheless, a horse or bird can do one essential thing a car or plane cannot: think on its own, at least to some extent.
What is the origin of the products or methods you use?	Improvement in many areas of engineering is now more likely to be incremental rather than revolutionary. But in other areas, notably automation and intelligence, the seeds of revolution are clearly visible.
Does the flowchart for the process resemble any other processes?	Network routing is at the heart of an airline's operations. Can network thinking apply to cars as well?

In 2008, *Wired* magazine reported the story of Shai Agassi, who is leading an ambitious project to convert Israel to all-electric cars. The essential problem with electric cars has always been battery capacity. Rather than go with the mechanical metaphors that had dominated the car business, Agassi, a senior executive with software giant SAP, looked at the problem sidewise. According to *Wired*, "What Shai was building was still essentially a software company. He needed a network that allowed cars to tell the grid how much charge they were carrying and how much more they required. The system had to know where the car was, so it could tell the driver where to go to 'fill up.' And it had to electronically negotiate with the local energy utility over when it could and couldn't take power and how much to pay."

Thinking of a car company in software terms gives you creative insights about change that you can't get any other way. What if your software company were a car company? What if it's the Post Office (which we will be exploring in greater detail later in this chapter)? What business are you in? Before you think hardware—or software, for that matter—perhaps you should reframe and try again.

The "Nothing New Under the Sun" Technique

Today's speed of technological change is, we're repeatedly told, unprecedented in human history. Advancements in information transfer happen with dizzying speed, dooming inflexible minds to the bin of obsolescence. Well, *unprecedented* is a dangerous word where history is concerned. Bursts of rapid change, technological and otherwise, have often occurred in the past. Looking through their lens, we can sometimes see patterns where none are immediately apparent.

The "Nothing New Under the Sun" technique involves taking a historical business that's parallel to your own and using that study to help you see changes and patterns in your own business and project environment. So our next key question is: what business are you in? Table 9-3 will help.

Table 9-3. Find Your Business Analogy

To identify potential analogs to your business, product, or service, consider the following questions and what businesses they may identify.

Sample Questions	Potential Insights
What is your business, in its most basic terms? (State so as simply as possible.)	You may find yourself coming up with more than one answer. Is the business of Ford designing cars, making cars, selling cars, or making money? Each description may provide potential analogs.
How was the need met before your solution came along?	If there's a technology solution, what was done before technology? Did the need go unmet, or was there some other process? How it was done before may give you useful insights into how to improve or build on what you're doing today.
What is the origin of the products or methods you use?	If they were adapted from another business or service area, perhaps that other business has insights you can use.
Does the flowchart for the process resemble any other processes?	Whether the other processes are businesses, machines, or wholly unrelated systems, when processes have structural similarities, there's always something to learn.

Here's an example.

On May 10, 1869, the Transcontinental Railroad, a modern miracle of engineering and science of the age, opened for business. Nothing similar in scope and complexity had been completed anywhere in the world. It would take 25 years for the Canadian Pacific Railway to open and 30 years for the Trans-Siberian Railway to do so. Completion of the middle 1,880-mile segment of the Transcontinental Railroad connected rails between east and west, a continuous rail line from New York to San Francisco.

That's a big project by anybody's standards.

This railroad changed the face of America instantly. The impact on American commerce was immediate and swift. Before completion of the Transcontinental Railroad, a trip from New York to San Francisco took several months of hard travel, and the cost for the travel was over $1,000. Just seven days after the railroad's opening, a first-class ticket from New York to San Francisco cost just $150 and the trip took only seven days.

In a matter of months, transcontinental shipping of goods by wagon and ship dropped to near nothing. Postage for a first-class letter went from several dollars to just four cents. The idea of America's "manifest destiny," once considered a pipe dream, was becoming reality.

From our creative project management perspective, what could we learn about today's projects from a study of the Transcontinental Railroad? What's the best parallel? Superhighways are one possible parallel; shipping lanes another. Or the network of air traffic corridors. Maybe a good parallel would be large infrastructure projects.

How about comparing the Transcontinental Railroad to the Internet? Do those two appear to be similar at all? Well, the Internet is sometimes referred to as the "information superhighway," and we've established that superhighways are similar to a rail network, so perhaps it's not so far-fetched an analogy after all. Like the Internet, our railroad moves packets (railcars) along a network, moving from switching yard to switching yard, until it reaches its destination.

The mere ability to draw a parallel doesn't automatically mean the parallel is useful. However, if you look at the evolution of the rail industry in the late nineteenth century, you'll find a pattern of boom and bust quite similar to the turbulence in the high-tech world in the late twentieth and early twenty-first centuries. You'll see a political cycle as well, with the railroads starting off as a high-tech oddity, growing to become the tax-advantaged darlings hailed as the saviors of America, then slowly turning into villains in the news media.

Sort of like Microsoft or Google.

The First Internet

Finding the right business analog is not easy. What is the business you're really in?

One of the biggest fields that uses project management is information technology. If you're in that field, and that's the subject area of your projects, you might want to look at how your company and profession are likely to evolve. So let's continue to use IT as an example. The Transcontinental Railroad is one analog, as we've seen. What is another?

If the Internet is a tool to send packets of information through pipes to routers, and from routers eventually to their final destination, we can see how the Transcontinental Railroad relates, but there's a better example: the most important high-tech institution in American life. We're talking, naturally, about the United States Post Office Department—nowadays the United States Postal Service.

Today, it's dismissed as "snail mail," but regular mail delivery was one of the great technological breakthroughs of the modern age. It built a mammoth organization with immense power and reach, a vital center of public life, an institution simultaneously loved and distrusted—in short, the Google of its day. It appears strange to the modern reader that Benjamin Franklin, the greatest mind of the Revolutionary era, would take a job like postmaster general in the new American government. The position seems rather small.

The reality was very much otherwise. Franklin was an outstanding organizer and manager who had revolutionized the chaotic colonial post system established by the British. More than 20 years before the start of the American Revolution, Benjamin Franklin had worked his way up from postmaster of Philadelphia to be joint postmaster general for the British-American colonies. (He was fired in 1774 for involvement in revolutionary activities.) During his tenure, he personally inspected 1,600 miles of rudimentary post roads and post offices. He established what was the FedEx service of its day—a weekly mail wagon between Philadelphia and Boston. Relays of riders kept the wagon moving day and night, cutting travel time in half.

The American colonies were sparsely populated and spread out over a huge geographic expanse. Infrastructure was spotty at best. Regular mail was the essential tool that allowed a revolutionary movement to form a new nation, and regular mail was the only institution that was able to hold it together. Franklin took over the reins of the single largest institution in the country, oversaw the acquisition and merger into the new government, and left a dynamic and powerful entity at the cutting edge of every technological advance of the nineteenth century. Among the developments were the following:

■ **Moving packets.** Packets of information flowed along the branches of that era's version of the information superhighway (i.e., dirt roads often built by the Post Office), reaching various nodes, where the packets were sorted by address label, sent to other nodes, and eventually reached the intended recipient. Today's information travels by twisted-pair copper wire, by fiber optic cable, by microwave, and by WiFi. Postal packets traveled in wagons, on horseback, and by water. In some places, postal packets went on skis, by balloon, or via carrier pigeon. Often, mail waited in general stores for rural delivery customers to call—sort of like an Internet café.

■ **Government efficiency.** The United States Post Office Department was arguably the most important function of government at the time—like snow removal for the mayor of Chicago. More than any other government activity, the Post Office was a model of technological far-sightedness and management excellence.

■ **Technology and pioneers.** The Post Office invested heavily in new technology, and adapted outside technology to improve delivery of the mails. A proposed urban pneumatic system ended up in shambles, much like Denver International Airport's fabled baggage system, but steady progress in automation and systems engineering paid dividends. Efficiency and speed steadily increased.

The Post Office continually expanded into new technologies and new service areas to fulfill its mandate of delivering the entire nation's letters. It became the nation's largest retail consumer banker, offering a full line of money orders along with savings accounts. During its epic expansion, the Post Office made powerful enemies who accused it of evil business practices. Rural merchants lobbied Congress to keep the Post Office out of small package delivery, fearing an end to their captive market. It was not until 1915 that the Post Office was able to deliver consumer goods. It's no coincidence that Montgomery Ward and Sears enjoyed their most explosive growth after that date.

■ **What happened to the Post Office of old?** What removed the Post Office from its preeminent place in American life was the same thing that put it there: new technology. Mail delivery originally began and for millennia remained a government function to maintain supremacy over the empire. Most ancient empires of any stature had some sort of mail service; letters and decrees had to be distributed effectively to reach all the corners of the empire. However the sheer logistical and technological difficulty of the job limited the mail to official business, with some space for personal correspondence of rulers and aristocrats. Julius Caesar, for example, was a prolific correspondent, often dictating to three separate scribes while he was riding on horseback.

The collapse of the Roman mail system contributed to the collapse of the Roman world, and communities fell into relative isolation because they were no longer on the network. The revival and expansion of mail was one of the glorious inventions of the Renaissance. But at the high water mark of mail—as frequently happens with technology—new media began to appear.

What does that have to do with us? Let's look at the information technology leaders in American history: the Post Office, AT&T, IBM, Microsoft, and now Google. Are there patterns here? Is there a common organizational life cycle?

As with any analogy, it's dangerous to draw conclusions that are too literal and too specific, but there's a lot of good information to be had. This can help you plan your organization's future, or at least know what to expect when things change.

When Your Business Goes Away

Projects are ways to close gaps, but that means you have to recognize a gap when it appears.

When a weekly mail wagon could get your letter from Philadelphia to Boston so quickly you could expect a reply in under a month, urgent messages traveled by mail wagon and the senders were grateful. When the telegraph came along, an entire class of messages switched from the existing medium of mail to the new medium of copper wire. The Post Office might have gone for a hostile acquisition strategy and gobbled up Western Union. (Something like that happened in other countries; in the United States, the Post Office was legally forbidden to enter the telegraph business.) But even that wouldn't change the technological fact that a certain amount of mail had gone away, and it wasn't coming back.

When you could pick up the phone and talk with someone in real time, another batch of mail (and quite a few telegraph messages) switched over to the new technology on the block. Long distance seemed an unassailable fortress for the Postal Service to conquer—the "Ma Bell" fears of the 1960s seem particularly quaint in retrospect—but she, too, eventually yielded. The arrival of e-mail has dramatically continued to reduce first-class mail volume for the U.S. Postal Service. Phone service, once technology's proudest telecommunications triumph, is now called POTS (plain old telephone service), and it is bundled with higher margin services whenever possible.

There's a pattern at work here, and it's no secret: it's the "creative destruction" that animates capitalism. In spite of this, organizations—and all too many projects—continue to rationalize and justify current practices of the existing business model even as it is imploding under the press of continuing progress. Notice that revolutionary change has reached the mail business before, not least by the Post Office Department itself. However, each wave of change provides the same set of options and decisions:

- Can the new technology help us do our business better?

- Does the new technology take away any current business?

- Does the new technology solve needs we don't address?

- What could we do to meet new customer needs, with or without the new technology?

- Should we acquire the new technology for ourselves?

Today, messages that once would have traveled first class mail now travel through other media and other carriers. Bill paying is in the process of migrating to the Internet. At least some direct advertising resources are shifting away from mail. What should the Post Office do?

The answers vary, but the questions stay the same.

Is your business in danger of being swept away? Notice that cognitive biases sometimes put managers and customers in denial, but it's vital for you to see the handwriting on the wall.

How to Develop Creative Solutions

Admiral William Halsey Jr., commander of the U.S. Third Fleet during World War II, famously established a "Department of Dirty Tricks," whose job it was to create innovative ideas to disrupt the enemy. We're not encouraging dirty tricks or unethical practices for managing projects in this book. We do, however, advocate uncovering creative solutions for any project management problem.

Schedule routine sessions throughout the project life cycle to ask the questions and use the tools provided in this book. You'll find the thought exercise clears cognitive cobwebs out of the mind of the team, and it helps identify what the team may be missing or if biases or assumptions need to be reassessed. Don't limit brainstorming to your own team or to a single group of people. Bring in outsiders; they'll see things insiders miss.

Table 9-4 gives some good questions to stimulate your creative process.

Table 9-4. Tools for Identifying and Responding to Sudden Change

Sample Questions	Tools or Processes You Might Use
What things are true now but may not remain true?	Negative brainstorming, fishbone
What is the biggest issue we are facing right this minute that could trigger a catastrophe?	Seven Level Outcome Evaluation (definitions failure and catastrophe)
If our mission failed, what would we have to do to clean it up and close it down?	Contingency planning, triage analysis

In the everyday real world, if your vision appears to be blocked, first make sure your eyes aren't closed, and then look for other ways to figure out what's going on. You might look around a corner, or use a mirror, or set up a video feed, or climb a ladder. You could use x-rays or ultrasound, radar or sonar, possibly night-vision goggles. You could also probe by inference and analogy.

Then you'll have the power to come up with powerful creative answers.

When Your Needs Are Contradictory

We've talked about industries as a whole. Now, let's narrow the focus down to a smaller historical parallel and show you how you can find whole new project opportunities through the right kind of framing.

At the American International Toy Fair in New York City one year—the year the Cabbage Patch Kids were the hot new toy—one of the authors of this book and his boss at the time, a former Hasbro executive, were standing in a knockoff importer showroom looking at "Broccoli Patch Kids."

"You know," the boss said, "there's actually a brilliant Cabbage Patch knockoff at this show. But it's not what you think. You've got to understand what the retailer wants. A hit product has to be brand new and completely original, or customers won't come looking for it. And it has to be just like everything else, or the retailer won't be able to merchandise it."

Contradictory needs are a big problem on projects, and the average project manager throws up his or her hands. "How can it be brand new and original *and* just like everything else?"

The answer is framing, and for framing, you need creativity. If you'll recall, the essential gimmick of Cabbage Patch Kids was that they could be adopted. Each doll was slightly different, and each came with a "birth certificate." Changing the vegetable from cabbage to broccoli adds nothing. The correct framing question is "what else could you adopt?"

Well, how about pets from the pound?

Pound Puppies, a very successful brand, takes the adoption idea from Cabbage Patch Kids (it's just like everything else), but it changes the concept from babies to pets. (It's brand new and completely original.)

Frame the problem correctly, and it's much easier to find the creative solution.

Paradoxes, Real and Apparent

Let's take this a step farther. If the requirements are contradictory, it looks like you're trapped in a paradox.

When you confront an apparent paradox, all too frequently the obvious move is to disregard it. After all, how can you resolve a contradiction? Sometimes, you can't. But other times, the paradox is only an illusion. It appears irresolvable; therefore, it discourages us from even looking or considering alternatives. When you are able to identify a paradoxical requirement or need, it may be an opportunity, not a threat.

What, for example, would a perfect product test look like? A perfect test provides an honest, complete evaluation—and never fails any products. It's an apparent paradox. But let's look deeper and reframe our perspective. We don't want to cheat on the quality of testing because we need to know that the product or service is of good quality. Inadequate testing can result in injury and litigation. However, we don't really want things to fail testing, because it's costly to do the rework.

Can these apparently contradictory aims be resolved?

Sure. That's what the quality movement is all about. Techniques like statistical process control, developed by Walter Shewhart of Western Electric in the 1920s, identify special causes of variation when they occur, instead of waiting until final testing. By the time the product gets to the final inspection stages, few if any defects remain to be discovered.

Whenever the decision is presented as "either-or," make sure you explore the possibility of "both-and." Just because it looks like a paradox doesn't mean there isn't an answer. Reframing the apparent contradiction sometimes holds the secret to success.

Making Great Bad Decisions

If we can't resolve our personal Cabbage Patch paradox and find a way around the dilemma, then we have to make a bad decision. Choosing between bad and worse is arguably more difficult than choosing between bad and good.

In the classic movie *Butch Cassidy and the Sundance Kid,* Butch and Sundance are both trapped on the edge of the cliff with a posse in close pursuit. It's time for a meeting of the project team to discuss risk response options. Butch starts off by clarifying the project gap. He says: "The way I look at it, we can either fight or give. If we give, we go to jail. If we fight, they can go for position and shoot us, wait and starve us out, maybe start a rock slide and get us that way. What else can they do?"

"They could surrender to us, but I wouldn't count on it," replies the Kid.

Butch thinks for a minute. "Wait! We'll jump!" It's 300 feet down into rock-filled, treacherous waters. And after some argument (and Sundance's painful admission, "I can't swim!"), both men eventually jump.

What kind of idiot makes a blind 300-foot death-defying leap into uncharted waters? Answer: the one who's otherwise dead anyway.

Making good decisions is easy. A good decision implies the existence of a good alternative, and anybody can do that. If there is a good choice, problem solved. But what if all your alternatives are rotten? In most organizations, the decision gets kicked up the ladder. The higher you are, the nastier the choices that end up on your desk.

Actually, Butch and Sundance had a pretty easy choice: the certainty of death, if they stayed; the probability of death, if they jumped. Not a pleasant decision, but not a hard one. Real leaders have it worse. They have to choose among strategies each of which makes sense given a specific future. But they don't know what the future is going to bring.

There's an art in making good bad decisions, and it's arguably one of the most important leadership characteristics, both in and out of project management. The goal of creative project managers is to slip out of the dilemma whenever possible.

If you can't avoid a bad decision, it's important to choose boldly. Being wishy-washy or wimping out on the dilemma almost always makes things worse.

Ptolemy and Project Management

All books on project planning necessarily describe planning as a set of linear steps, even if those steps fall into a three-stroke PMBOK Plan-

Execute-Monitor/Control or a Deming four-stroke cycle of Plan-Do-Study-Act.

While in theory the process is fairly straightforward, in practice the reality is much messier, because project management is Ptolemaic. To give you an idea of what we mean by Ptolemaic, let's take a look at some astronomical phenomena. As we sweep around the sun, we sometimes pass our neighbors riding in the interplanetary slow lanes. From our earthly perspective, the other planets appear to slow, stop, and then move backward in their heavenly orbits, a phenomenon known as retrograde motion. To the ancient Greek scholar Ptolemy, who believed in a fixed Earth at the center of the universe, this was a puzzle. After careful thought, he concluded that the motion of the planets went in epicycles, a circular looping pattern like something made by an old spiral drawing toy. The Ptolemaic system of epicycles and celestial spheres tried to account for everything, but instead grew insanely complex, eventually yielding to Copernicus, who cut the Gordian knot by moving the center of the solar system from Earth to the sun.

Ptolemaic—that's what "iterative" looks like in practice.

We don't get to follow the process of managing a project directly from A to B, from input to output. Instead, each new step often opens our eyes to issues best resolved in earlier steps. You advance in a dizzying loop in which you can't always tell if the net momentum is forward or back. The discipline of "agile" project management is increasingly popular in project management because it addresses the iterative nature of many projects, especially in creative or research disciplines.

But even if your Gantt chart resembles a textbook "waterfall" development process (each task on the time line flows into the next, like water flowing down a series of steps), there's still agile Brownian motion going on underneath that can shift the tectonic plates on which your project rests.

No matter how important planning is, the project plan is not the project. There's only so much time available, and for better or worse, you have to go to work. Some issues get swept under the rug of cognitive bias, others do not. But we must and do move on. People change, technology changes, and sometimes the underlying issues themselves mutate with the passage of time. Sometimes it's a slow drift, other times a hard right turn.

We've all had the experience of being caught off guard by sudden change. That will happen occasionally no matter what you do. Some things aren't just unknown; they're unknowable—often until it's too late. Nevertheless, the creative project manager must continuously probe that outer darkness with the certain knowledge that disruptive forces are ever present. It is better to seek out and respond to issues on their terms rather than react in crisis mode on someone else's.

10

Salvaging Project Value

Sometimes I am a collector of data, and only a collector, and am
likely to be gross and miserly, piling up notes, pleased with merely
numerically adding to my stores. Other times I have joys, when
unexpectedly coming upon an outrageous story that may not be
altogether a lie, or upon a macabre little thing that may make some
reviewer of my more or less good works mad. But always there
is present a feeling of unexplained relations of events that I note,
and it is this far-away, haunting, or often taunting, awareness,
or suspicion, that keeps me piling on.
—Charles Fort, *Wild Talents*, 1932

Closing Time

The closeout of a project is too often taken for granted. Take a look at the
average project plan: the official end of the project is the completion of
the work. Obviously, that's an important milestone, but it's not really the
end of the project.

Project closeout is an essential stage in the project life cycle—and
there's a lot of creativity involved in running a great closeout. If you don't
take it seriously enough to include it as a work package in your project
network diagram, you're likely to miss certain details. Not paying enough
attention causes problems, and one of the saddest causes of project failure
is an improper or incomplete closeout.

There are four minimum steps required to finish a project properly:

1. **Complete.** When you have done the operational work necessary to close the gap, the work is complete.

2. **Turned over.** After the work is complete, it must be converted to its useful state and turned over to the people now responsible for its operation and maintenance. When those people have accepted the work, it officially has been turned over.

3. **Closed out.** After the work is turned over, there are various administrative tasks necessary for wrapping up the project. Final invoices, internal paperwork, procurements, documentation, files—each organization and each project has its own level of need. The project is closed out when the administrative work is complete and properly archived.

4. **Value captured.** Every project, whether an outstanding success or catastrophic failure, has value that needs extracting. Lessons learned are one such value, and there may be others as well. The project has had its value captured when its indirect benefits reach the appropriate stakeholders.

In practice, most project teams concentrate solely on reaching "complete," and perhaps "turned over," although project managers often don't bother to figure out what that means until late in the project. Apparently, they figure that the other steps will take care of themselves. Unfortunately, they often don't.

Over the course of the project, resources are reallocated and overhead costs redistributed, and at the end there's no obvious requirement for a first-rate project closeout. Everybody's moving on to new challenges by that time, anyway.

Closeout becomes the least of the worries.

Looking at the Essential Steps to Project Closeout

Each of these essential steps needs to be treated as a work package in project planning. Notice that the steps of "complete" and "turned over" must be achieved before the deadline, but the steps of "closed out" and "value captured" can legitimately take place after the deadline.

Complete

Work complete should, at a minimum, be considered a major milestone, but it's not necessarily or automatically the end of the project.

Certain issues tend to rise in seriousness toward the end of the project. If your project has run for several years, there may have been multiple staffing changes since the project's inception. The team that started the project is no longer in place. Team members now are dealing with assumptions, projections, and budgets they did not develop. This is also a time when smoldering personality conflicts can resurface as the team reviews specific performance issues. Finally compounding the personnel issues, key members of the team may be reassigned to new projects, causing a loss of their perspective and increasing the workload for remaining team members.

Any issues that might have been addressed earlier in the project will tend to land here, on the grounds that if the person carrying the grievance waited any longer, his or her concerns would be moot. If there's a negative stakeholder, you should anticipate some last-minute resistance.

Turned Over

The time to think about effective project turnover is during the early planning stages. What physical document of your results will you turn over? To whom will you turn it over? When will that be? Will there be any follow-up responsibilities expected? Should there be? Which side will handle what parts of the transition?

There are many different types of transitions, as Table 10-1 shows.

Table 10-1. Types of Turnovers

Turnover	Description	Issues
Over the wall	A stage of the work or of the process is completed and handed over to another department or organization.	How will quality problems be avoided during handoffs?
Maintenance	The project is finished, but the department that managed the project is also responsible for use or operation.	How does the project transition into its service and operational role?
Cyclic	The project goes through updates, upgrades, or repeat cycles. A project team reconvenes periodically for the next cycle.	How can the value of the operational experience be leveraged?
Manufacturing	The project developed a product or process that operates on an industrial scale.	Who is the owner of the manufacturing process? How will maintenance, upgrades, and training take place?

Closing Out

The creative approach to the technical and administrative functions of closeout is how to get it done in the simplest and easiest way possible. Closeout is a necessary headache. The best strategy for proceeding with it is to set up a file folder or other receptacle for closeout materials at the beginning of the project. Doing so will save you the trouble of having to round up a few hundred pieces of scattered paper while you're scrambling to finish a thousand other tasks near the project's end.

Recovering Value

The first three parts of closing out a project are mandatory, but, alas, no matter how valuable lessons learned are, you are by no means *required* to learn lessons from any endeavor you undertake. As W. Edwards Deming said, "It is not necessary to change. Survival is not mandatory."

Survival, indeed, is not mandatory—but it's highly desirable. If you don't learn the lessons each project teaches, you're at high risk of failing to survive in project management.

Every authority in the field of project management agrees how essential lessons learned really are. There's a reason, however, why this section is headlined "Recovering Value" rather than "Lessons Learned" (the more traditional formulation): there's a big problem with lessons learned as practiced in the great majority of organizations.

Here's what typically happens.

- We don't do lessons learned at all.

- We do learn, but we focus on who's to blame, not on how to avoid the problem in the future.

- We make sure we don't learn any lessons that sound like we're criticizing the boss.

- We write a report, and nobody reads it.

- We check "lessons learned" off our to-do list.

Perhaps the problem is with the name itself. "Lessons learned" sounds like a session with the high school principal, and no matter how many spoonfuls of sugar, the medicine just doesn't want to go down. Let's be creative and think of it from a new angle: recovering value from the project.

That involves a lot more than just learning lessons.

There are many fine resources on how to lead and manage lessons learned processes, and we don't need to duplicate well-trod ground. What's wrong with lessons learned is not what's there, but what's not there.

Lessons learned are a way to extract value from a project that can be used beneficially on future work. That's a good way to extract value. But it's not the only way. You can take your team farther if you reframe the process as "recovering value," with "lessons learned" being only one of the processes you should follow.

The Extraction Process

Raw wool requires careful cleaning to eliminate dirt, oil, and foreign matter. In the process it becomes thicker, or fuller. A particularly good solvent for treating wool, historically, was urine, human and otherwise. The urine business (collection, processing, and distribution) was so lucrative, ancient Rome levied a special tax on commercial-grade urine, paid by the barrel.

On a more pleasant note, organizations that develop lots of photographs, especially x-rays, accumulate wastewater filled with silver. The wastewater needs to be purified, and the recovered silver has some value.

One person's wastewater is another person's treasure. But to gain the value of that treasure, you have to process an awful lot of wastewater.

What are you wasting in your project? Look at the following four areas to find extractable value:

1. **Incidental value.** A byproduct that turns out to have value in its own right
2. **Operational value.** The value of the process and tools you developed in making the product
3. **Political value.** The reputation and relationship benefits produced by the project
4. **Benchmarks.** How much, how long, how hard the project was, and what that augurs for future projects

Incidental Value

Projects often create significant incidental value, but a lot of that value doesn't pay off unless it's recognized and exploited. Looking for value in unexpected places can pay great dividends. Sometimes even failed projects yield value. For example, consider the Leaning Tower of Pisa. The city fathers of Pisa were devastated to see their great tower settle at an angle. It was a colossal failure in terms of its original project objectives. But if that tower didn't lean, how many people would bother to visit it?

A 3M scientist, Dr. Spencer Silver, accidentally developed a "low-tack" adhesive in 1968. Nobody could figure out anything useful to do with it until 1974 when a colleague, Art Fry, used the adhesive to anchor a bookmark in his hymnbook. In 1977, a market test of the concept failed. 3M tried again a year with a massive free samples campaign, and by 1980 Post-it Notes were a major product line.

Go through the trash. As part of recovering value from the project, take all the project paper—scraps, meeting notes, junk, drafts, whatever—and have the team go through it, selecting anything of value and getting rid of the rest. (But check your organization's document disposal guidelines first.)

If you performed tests or experiments and have leftover early versions of ones that failed to work, go through the results to see if there is any secondary value, then file or destroy them as appropriate.

Operational Value

General Ulysses S. Grant famously said, "It is well and wise to learn from our mistakes, but I prefer to learn from the mistakes of others."

Forget what went right or what went wrong for a minute. Focus instead on *what you did*: the work packages, the action steps, the processes used. Reconstruct the network diagram and time line based on what actually happened.

Sometimes a project is truly unique, and you'll find yourself blazing a new trail. But most of the time you'll find yourself doing the same things on one project that you did on others, so it makes sense to have some systems and procedures in place to streamline the work. Developing templates, forms, checklists, processes, and other tools to streamline repetitive tasks is one of the most powerful benefits project management can give you. Most people leave all that value on the table and end up reinventing the wheel on every single project.

Risk management benefits from this kind of operational analysis. After a while, you see patterns. As we noted earlier, sometimes it's one thing after another, but usually it's the same thing over and over again. When you know something is likely to happen, you can prepare for it.

Political Value

In Chapter 7, we talked about the importance of having an effective intelligence operation with respect to your project environment. You need to extract the political value from the project as well. You may need to do this in the privacy of your own mind. What did you learn about the behavior and reactions of other people? Their strengths and weaknesses? How can you influence them in a positive manner? How do you want to position them with respect to future projects? What do they need to learn or change in order to be more successful?

Benchmarks

In our varied leaps through project management space and time, we've taken free advantage of 20/20 hindsight. We already know how most of the stories turned out, and that helps us no end in drawing useful lessons.

Companies often use business case studies as a means of improving performance. We've used stories from history to provide a fresh perspective on business issues. The Ford Pinto case is taught so often because it offers a variety of lessons and insights, while reminding participants of the potential for catastrophe in apparently straightforward projects. It doesn't matter whether your organization makes cars or not. Similarly, few of us will be running major military operations like Eisenhower or Patton, but all of us make decisions, deal with unruly subordinates, and deal with confusing and unclear data.

There are four basic goals in evaluating our project experience:

1. Learn from the project experience.
2. Find underlying causes for problems.
3. Offer suggestions to correct problems.
4. Minimize problems on future projects.

With the Ford Pinto case, the project involved developing an inexpensive automobile. The design team had a very specific mission: design a car to be produced and sold for less than $2,000. They accomplished their stated goal and threw the design over the wall to the next group. The safety issue had been flagged, but it was someone else's problem.

Achieving your goal isn't automatically the same thing as closing the gap. "We had to destroy the village in order to save it" qualifies as a barely adequate result, at best.

Perfect Lessons Learned

In our Seven Level Outcome Evaluation tool, we identified the level of perfect, a project outcome that involves no compromises or trade-offs, and fulfills all customer expectations, hopes, and dreams. It's best to evaluate the project you and your team have just completed by asking, "If we had perfect foreknowledge and access to all available resources, how would we have done this project differently?" Framing the questions this way eliminates a good deal of the potential negativity. What did you learn about the gap or the objective late in the project that would have been helpful to know earlier? The fact that it might not have been possible to know isn't really at issue.

You might wonder how it's useful to pretend as if you had knowledge and power that you really didn't have at the time. The advantage comes because you're looking at the future, not the past. Yes, perhaps you could not have known that a particular event would happen. But is there a way you could use your newfound awareness to put yourself in a more advantageous position in a similar situation in the future?

Scaling the Process

Some level of lessons learned is essential if you want to improve the way you manage future projects or develop yourself as a project manager (see Table 10-2). That being said, not every examination needs to turn into a forensic autopsy.

Table 10-2. Levels of Lessons Learned

Level	Description	Circumstances	Cost
Quick and dirty	Perform a cursory review of key project elements: Was it completed? Was the customer satisfied? What were the big issues? What would we do differently next time?	Use for smaller, less important projects, or for one-shot undertakings that are unlikely to be repeated.	Very low
Standard	Conduct a formal meeting with a process agenda; keep detailed records; issue a report.	Use for projects of significant scope and cost and projects performed on a routine basis.	Once a standard has been developed, cost is low to moderate.
Full-court press	Do a comprehensive audit of an entire project, normally for the purpose of standardizing procedures and approaches, and for performing comprehensive risk analysis.	Use for projects that are repeated often, where development of standard approaches and risk contingency plans is of particularly high value.	Very high cost; high potential value

To make meaningful lessons learned on your project, you must plan for them in the beginning. Using Table 10-2, decide what level of effort and potential value is likely to result from lessons learned, using the size of the project and the frequency with which it is repeated as guidelines. A truly comprehensive lessons learned process is a significant investment of resources. It's not necessary to go that far on every project.

Identify and protect resources for this process, and establish early how the information needed for the lessons learned process will be collected and organized. Memories are subject to cognitive bias and to general fading; without objective data, there's a limited amount of evaluation possible. The goal of the project review is to facilitate and codify what's been learned for use in future projects. Since projects have beginning goals and a final outcome, analyzing the difference can be very revealing.

Guidelines for Standard Lessons Learned Reviews

Here are some specific techniques for conducting closeout session focused on the technical and administration aspects of the project:

- Conduct a session within two to three weeks after the project turnover.

- Include as many participants or representatives of various functions as possible. Be sure to include individuals who may have left the project or had part-time involvement.

- Gather a wide spectrum of specialties and seniority to benefit from diverse perspectives.

- Develop a time line to guide discussions for each phase of the project to prevent the discussion concentrating on just the most recent events, which might result in overlooking specific parts of the project.

- Select and distribute the agenda well in advance; include specific expectations for information to bring to the meeting(s) and meeting outcomes.

If you're electing a full-court press, add these guidelines:

- Utilize an off-site location, if possible, or a neutral location within the organization.

- Utilize the services of an independent facilitator, if possible.

Adherence to these guidelines is a good start for establishing an effective 360-degree coverage of lessons learned.

Individual Team Member Project Lessons Learned

Challenge yourself and members of your team to perform your own personal lessons learned. Each member can do part of this process alone; the goal is to learn the lessons you personally need, regardless of anyone else. Share your insights, if you're comfortable doing so; don't force others to do the same. Ask yourself:

- Did we challenge our assumptions sufficiently to anticipate emerging performance issues?

- How successfully did we manage our cognitive biases?

- How effectively did we help promote open discussion to challenge group bias and assumptions? If it was not done so effectively, how can we improve?

- How did we respond to challenges from the group when they were offering alternative opinions?

- What did we miss, and why?

- Why were we wrong? What can we do differently next time?

And in the End . . .

Project closeout is more than the administrative actions required to close contracts, complete financial documents, or reassign project personnel. Project closeout offers the opportunity to harvest the knowledge gained during the project.

Many organizations have invested heavily in project management training, personnel development processes, and associated hardware and software. They have not successfully harvested the knowledge from specific projects to recycle and leverage newfound capabilities. Practices and processes that hinder performance are being inadvertently continued because they have not been identified as detrimental to performance. Project closeout offers both the organization and the individual the opportunity to learn and grow. While traditional project closeout reviews focus on process and methodology, creative project managers put extra attention on the cognitive biases, perceptions, and interpersonal issues that often cause far more damage. Table 10-3 compares the traditional with the individual.

Table 10-3. Comparison of Project and Individual Reviews

Traditional Project Closeout Review	Individual Project Review
Administrative requirements	What cognitive biases affect this project environment?
Performance information	What kinds of blind spots do I have?
Environmental issues	What if I am wrong?
Process review	What am I not seeing?
Formal acceptance	What questions should I be asking?
Historical documentation	How effectively are we communicating?

The Dangerous Game

As mentioned, 70 percent of projects fail in one way or another. While some project managers finish the Game of Life in Millionaire Acres, others become untouchables in the company caste system, and everything in between. Project managers would do well to remember the motto of Jay Ward's cartoon character Superchicken (he was on the *George of the Jungle* TV show), whose refrain was "You knew the job was dangerous when you took it!"

If you didn't know when you started, you surely know by now.

Becoming an outstanding project manager is a lifelong journey. Gandhi and Patton both spent many years learning their trade before they entered their great years. So did Sewell Avery and Ignaz Semmelweis, and both men failed.

The difference is in how they thought. Gandhi and Patton, different in so many ways, shared a creative spirit. Both were willing to see outside their own traditional paradigms and the biases of others. Avery and Semmelweis, on the other hand, were ruined because of their failure to see what was really going on.

Ultimately, there are no magic solutions. Creative project management is about this mindset above all. Creativity is a skill. As with any other skill, practice and hard work form the road to success. Remember Thomas Edison: it's 1 percent inspiration, 99 percent perspiration.

As you know, he got good results.

Join the conversation on our blog at sidewiseinsights.blogspot.com.

Appendix A

Questions for the
Creative Project Manager

Computers are useless. They can only give you answers.
—Pablo Picasso, 1968

THROUGHOUT THIS BOOK, we've listed a large number of potential questions to help challenge your thinking about any project. Obviously, there are far too many questions to deal with at any one time, and that's fine. Some questions will have more bearing on some projects than on others. Keep in mind that it's always good to have an unusual question to throw in whenever a meeting seems to be running into the fog of bias.

With that, here is our list of questions.

Project Fundamentals

- Why are we doing this?

- Who has an interest in what we're doing, and what do they each want and need?

- What do we have to do? How are we going to do it?

- Who needs to be involved? In what way?

Assessing Difficulty and Cognitive Bias

- What makes this project difficult?

- What aren't we seeing correctly—or at all?

- How will people react to this project?

- What if I'm wrong?

- What am I not seeing? How are my cognitive biases distorting my judgment?

Understanding the Gap

- What's the gap between where we are and where we want to be—official, underlying, and hidden? How might the gap change?

- What's the project, and how does it relate to the gap?

- What is the minimum necessary decision and action I must perform *right now*?

- What other projects are going on around me?

- How should I define the end or goal of the immediate project?

- How should I triage the work?

- How will I manage constraints, complexity, and uncertainty?

Outcome Evaluation

- How good is "good enough"? How do I define the other six outcome levels?

■ What's the lowest level of performance achievable without extraordinary effort?

■ What's the desired level of performance that will close the gap that led to the project in the first place?

■ What are the events that could trigger catastrophe?

■ What are the opportunities available in perfection?

When It Appears Impossible

■ Does the project appear to be impossible? Why? Can constraints be modified, or can creativity overcome the barriers? Does the project need to be terminated?

■ Where is the box? What are its borders? Are they real? Are they flexible?

■ What's our biggest weakness?

■ If there's competition or opposition, what's the best and finest quality of the other side?

■ What's the craziest thing we could do?

■ What cognitive biases do we and our opponents have that might create blind spots?

Managing Constraints

■ How can we manage cost?
  • Is cash a flexible resource?
  • Do we have contingency funds to draw on?
  • Is there an acceptable or expected degree of normal budget overrun?

- Can we go back to the well?
- Is there someone else who can or should pay part of the bill?
- Are there flexible resources available?
- Can we borrow staff, equipment, or consumables?
- Can we borrow from other client deliverables?
- Are there resources with costs that aren't being charged to our project?
- Can we exploit intangible resources (call in favors, etc.)?
- Do we have project sponsors or key stakeholders who can help?

- How can we manage time?
  - Can we delay to acquire the authority to spend money in subsequent budget cycles?
  - Can we delay to improve quality or solve problems?
  - Can we schedule delay to coincide with resource availability?
  - Could delay lead to lower resource consumption during critical time periods?

- How can we manage performance?
  - Can we change grade?
  - Can we cut, modify, or substitute features?
  - Can we cut, modify, or adjust scope?
  - Will a partial delivery satisfy immediate customer needs?
  - Can we fix it or upgrade it later?

Environmental Analysis

- What are we assuming? What should we assume? When should we check our assumptions?

- What do we wish we had known earlier?

- What is happening in our environment?

- What are our strengths, weaknesses, opportunities, and threats?

- How do inertia, friction, and entropy affect our project choices?

- How can I get the power I need to accomplish our goals? How can I work with and share power with others to accomplish our goals?

- Am I confident no one will suffer a negative outcome from my behavior?

- Would I be pleased if other people used the same tactic to achieve their goals?

Managing People

- How do I manage my stakeholders?
  - Who is affected by the project positively, negatively, and tangentially? How much can they affect the project outcome?
  - What is the nature of the stakeholder interest? Is it process or product, core or peripheral? Are there personal or emotional issues involved?
  - What can be done to address the needs of this stakeholder? How can the stakeholder be positioned for best advantage to the project?
  - What care does the stakeholder require? How often and in what way do we need to communicate? Is the stakeholder's position or interest likely to change?

Managing Assumptions and Change

- What things are true now but may not remain true?

- What is the biggest issue we are facing right this minute that could trigger a catastrophe?

- If our mission failed, what would we have to do to clean it up and close it down?

- What business are we in?

- What's happening to our business?
  - What is our business, in its most basic terms, stated as simply as possible?
  - How was the need met before our solution came along?
  - What is the origin of the products or methods we use?
  - Does the flowchart for the process resemble any other processes?

Value Recovery and Lessons Learned

- What do we have to do to finish the project completely?

- What value can we recover in addition to completing the project?

- How can this project benefit us in the future?

- What can I personally learn from this experience?
  - Did I challenge my assumptions sufficiently to anticipate emerging performance issues?
  - How successfully did I manage my cognitive biases?
  - How effectively did I help promote open discussion to challenge group bias and assumptions? If I was relatively ineffective, how can I improve?
  - How did I respond to challenges from the group when offering alternative opinions?
  - What did I miss—and why?
  - Why was I wrong? What can I do differently next time?

Appendix B

Cognitive Biases

A

Actor-Observer Bias

This cognitive bias make us assume other people act the way they do because of their personality and not because of their situation. Do people steal food because they are immoral or because they are hungry? The real answer may vary; the bias is to assume the first.

When it comes to ourselves, the bias is reversed. We excuse our own behavior by citing our circumstances. Fight this bias in judging other people by focusing extra attention on their circumstances. Fight this bias in yourself by being aware of your own ethical choices.

Ambiguity Aversion Effect

Daniel Ellsberg, best known for releasing the Pentagon Papers in 1971, is also known for the 1962 discovery of the Ellsberg paradox, in which people make decisions, not because they are best, but because they seem less ambiguous.

To illustrate the Ellsberg paradox experiment with an example: Say that you have an urn with 30 red balls and 60 other balls that are either black or yellow. You don't know the ratio of black to yellow, only that the total of black and yellow is 60. You can make the following wagers:

- Gamble A: You get $100 if you draw a red ball.

- Gamble B: You get $100 if you draw a black ball.

You can also choose either of the following wagers (for another draw):

- Gamble C: You get $100 if you draw a red or a yellow ball.

- Gamble D: You get $100 if you draw a black or yellow ball.

If you prefer Gamble A to Gamble B, it's rational you should prefer Gamble C to Gamble D—the number of yellow balls is the same. If you prefer Gamble B to Gamble A, by similar logic you should prefer Gamble D to Gamble C.

But in actual surveys, most people strictly prefer Gamble A to Gamble B, and Gamble D to Gamble C. The logic that informs one decision breaks down for the other.

The idea of the ambiguity effect is that people prefer known risks over unknown risks, regardless of other factors. Choosing Gamble A over Gamble B is a preference for knowing the number of red balls, even though the number of black balls might be greater. Choosing Gamble D over Gamble C is a preference for knowing that the sum of black and yellow balls is 60, even if the sum of red and yellow might be greater.

Anchoring Effect

When people were asked the percentage of African nations that are members of the United Nations, people who were first asked, "Was it more or less than 45 percent?" gave lower estimates than those who were first asked, "Was it more or less than 65 percent?"

The numbers don't even have to be related. When an audience is first asked to write the last two digits of their Social Security numbers and then to submit mock bids in an auction, the half with the higher two-digit numbers submitted bids between 60 and 120 percent higher than those of the other half!

You can use the anchoring effect to your advantage in negotiations or sales situations. To combat it, be aware of any numbers mentioned and consciously try to disconnect them from your decision process.

Attentional Bias

If someone with cancer drinks green tea, and the cancer goes away, attentional bias might make someone conclude that drinking green tea cures cancer. After doing some research, it turns out that there are many cases in which someone who drank green tea also had a remission of cancer.

But that leaves out three other ideas that need to be tested: Have there been green tea drinkers whose cancer wasn't cured? Have there been people who didn't drink green tea whose cancer went into remission anyway? Is it the case that non–green tea drinkers always suffer fatal cancers?

Attentional bias happens when you focus on one piece of evidence and fail to examine different possible outcomes. To fight attentional bias, consciously list the various possibilities and make sure you analyze each one.

Availability Cascade

"Repeat something long enough and it will become true." Political operatives of all stripes take advantage of the availability cascade. Start with an idea that summarizes a complex situation in a simple, straightforward manner and you can start a chain reaction. The availability cascade is one of the processes that make up groupthink.

A variation on the availability cascade is to accuse others of falling victim to it to give the illusion that a minority position is in fact true. Both those who agree with the consensus on global warming and those who disagree with it accuse the other side of influencing the debate through this technique. However, it's important to distinguish between a consensus of popular opinion, which is heavily influenced by repetition, and a consensus of scientific opinion, which rests on a body of evidence. (One can challenge the evidence, of course, but that's a different kind of debate altogether.)

Availability Heuristic

If something's accessible in your memory, this cognitive bias causes you to think it's also more probable. In surveys, people think dying in a plane crash is more common than dying in a car crash, when it's the other way around. Plane crashes, of course, get more publicity.

A lot of racial or cultural stereotyping relies on the availability heuristic. "[Fill in the blank] steal a lot. I know, because a [fill in the blank] robbed my neighbor." Because a single close example stands out in memory, it seems probable that the characteristic is widespread, when of course a single case proves nothing one way or another.

B

Base Rate Fallacy

Suppose that there are 100 terrorists trying to sneak through airline security for every one million nonterrorists. The Transportation Security Administration (TSA) has set up an automated face recognition system that has a 99 percent accuracy rate. The alarm goes off, and trained Homeland Security agents swoop down. What is the probability that their captive is really a terrorist?

If the failure rate is 1 percent, that means there is a 99 percent chance the person is a terrorist and a 1 percent chance that he or she is not. Right? That justifies a significant assumption of guilt.

But this calculation actually gets it backward. The chance the person isn't a terrorist is far greater—in fact, it's 99.02 percent likely that the new prisoner is completely innocent!

The mistake that leads to the first conclusion is called the base rate fallacy. It occurs when you don't notice that the failure rate (1 in 100) is the not the same as the false alarm rate. The false alarm rate is completely different, because there are, after all, far more nonterrorists than terrorists. Let's imagine that we walk everyone—100 terrorists and one million nonterrorists, for a total of 1,000,100 people—in front of the face recognition tool. A 1 percent failure rate means it's going to ring incorrectly 1 time for each 100 passengers, 10,099 times in total. It will catch 99 terrorists and miss 1, but it's also going to catch 10,000 nonterrorists. The ratio is actually

99/10,099, or a miniscule 0.98 percent, that the person caught is actually a terrorist.

This does not argue against the value of screening. Screening might be perfectly reasonable. Overreaction, however, is not. If you're 99 percent sure you've caught a terrorist, you will behave differently than if you're only 1 percent sure.

To avoid the base rate fallacy, look at the "prior probability." If there were no terrorists, what would the face recognition system produce? With a 1 percent failure rate, it would never pick a real terrorist (there would be none), but it would trigger 10,000 false positives. Now you've found the missing fact.

Notice that the base rate fallacy only produces incorrect analysis when the scale is unbalanced, as is our case with 100 terrorists in city with a population of one million. As the populations approach 50/50, the fail ure rate and false alarm rate would converge. Mind you, we'd have differ ent problems then.

Belief Bias

Why is it so hard for our logical, well-reasoned arguments to penetrate other people's thick skulls? And, of course, why is it that people so seldom give logical, well-reasoned arguments to support their idiot ideas? Belief bias is the tendency for all of us to evaluate the logical strength of some-one's argument based on whether we believe in the truth or falsity of the conclusion. We're all subject to this one; susceptibility to belief bias is independent of reasoning ability.

The Red Queen in Lewis Carroll's *Through the Looking-Glass* prac-ticed believing five impossible things before breakfast, and that is not a bad exercise. Make sure you look at a diversity of information, and spend effort imagining how a reasonable person could reach a conclusion so different from your own. This isn't necessarily a recommendation for you to change your beliefs. But make sure your beliefs don't suffer from hard-ening of the mental arteries.

Bias Blind Spot

Bias blind spot is a recursive bias, the failure to compensate for one's own cognitive biases. For example, some 80 percent of drivers think they are substantially better than the average driver. That's called the "better-than-average effect." In such a situation, the vast majority of people think they are less subject to bias than the average person.

C

Choice-Supportive Bias

On a business trip to St. Thomas many years ago, the cab driver taking Michael back to the airport suddenly honked his horn at a car trying to pull out into traffic.

"Women drivers!" he said in disgust.

Michael looked over at the offending car. "Looks like the driver is male," Michael observed.

"Yeah, well, he drives like a woman," the cabbie replied.

Choice-supportive bias is the tendency to remember your choices as better than they are, to look for information that supports them, and reject information that does not. In the case of the St. Thomas cab driver, he's decided that women are bad drivers. Any time he sees a woman driving badly, he notices. When it's a man, he doesn't notice it's a man, or dismisses it as an anomaly ("He drives like a woman.").

This man doesn't think of himself as prejudiced, because he thinks the observed facts confirm his opinion. What he fails to see is that the key word is *observed*. He's blind to any facts that would challenge his opinion.

Choice-supportive bias is related to confirmation bias, the tendency to search for or interpret information to confirm one's own perceptions.

To fight choice-supportive bias in yourself, be skeptical of general beliefs you hold about people, groups, or the nature of life. There's probably important stuff you're overlooking.

Clustering Illusion

Is the sequence below random or nonrandom?

OXXXOXXXOXXOOOXOOXXOO

If you think the sequence looks nonrandom, you're with the majority—but you're wrong. The sequence has several characteristics of a random stream, an equal number of each result and an equal number of adjacent results. But people seem to expect a "random" sequence to have a greater number of alternations (O to X, or vice-versa) than statistics would predict. The chance of an alternation in a sequence of independent random binary events (e.g., flips of heads or tails on a coin) is 50 percent, but people seem to expect an alternation rate of about 70 percent.

The clustering illusion is a cognitive bias that creates a tendency to see patterns where none actually exist. This is why most people believe in "streaks." When you expect greater variation in a sequence, you tend to assume that there's a trend. But that isn't necessarily the situation.

Conjunction Fallacy

Linda is 31 years old, single, outspoken, and very bright. She majored in philosophy. As a student, she was deeply concerned with issues of discrimination and social justice, and also participated in antinuclear demonstrations.

Which statement is more probable?

1. Linda is a bank teller.
2. Linda is a bank teller and is active in the feminist movement.

In a 1982 study, 85 percent thought statement 2 was more probable than statement 1, but that's wrong. The probability of two events occurring together is always less than or equal to the probability of either one occurring alone. Even if there's a very low probability that Linda is a bank teller (let's make it 5 percent) and a very high probability that Linda is active in the feminist movement (say, 95 percent), the chance that Linda is a bank teller *and* active in the feminist movement is $5\% \times 95\%$, or 4.75%, lower than the probability of the first statement.

The conjunction fallacy happens when you assume that specific conditions are more probable than a single general one, which is a violation of basic logic. Now, one possibility is that because most people aren't familiar with the rules of formal logic, they may assume that statement 1 ("Linda is a bank teller") implies that she isn't active in the feminist movement. But the fallacy has been demonstrated with very educated audiences.

Another experiment by Tversky and Kahneman in the early 1980s surveyed a group of foreign policy experts to determine the probability that the Soviet Union would invade Poland and the United States would break off diplomatic relations with the Soviet Union in the following year. The consensus estimate was about a 4 percent chance. Next, another group of experts was asked the probability that the United States would break off relations with the Soviet Union the following year. They estimated only a 1 percent chance. This implies that the detailed, specific scenario provided to the first group of experts all by itself made the scenario seem more likely to happen.

Confirmation Bias

Evidence is seldom completely clean and clear. If a mass of facts argue against a position and one fact supports it, guess which fact we focus on? When confronted by a mass of data, we tend to be selective in the evidence we collect; we tend to interpret the evidence in a biased way; and when we recall evidence, we often do so selectively. This is why a search for facts isn't as persuasive as logic might suggest.

Congruence Bias

In congruence bias, you only test your hypothesis directly, potentially missing alternative explanations. In the famous Hawthorne experiment, Frederick W. Taylor, founder of scientific management, wanted to test whether improved lighting in factories would increase worker productivity. He performed a direct test: he measured productivity, installed better lighting, and measured productivity again. Productivity went up. If you are falling into congruence bias, you're done. Experiment confirmed; case closed.

But Taylor avoided the trap. He tested his hypothesis indirectly. If improved lighting increased productivity, he reasoned that worse lighting should lower it. So he tested that proposition as well. He took out a lot of lights and measured again: to everyone's surprise, productivity went up! A deeper analysis revealed what is now known as the Hawthorne effect: when people feel others are paying attention to them, their productivity tends to go up, at least temporarily. (It's a huge benefit of using management consultants; just by showing up, they are likely to make things better.)

To avoid congruence bias, don't be satisfied with direct reasoning alone. Direct confirmation asks, "If I behaved in accordance with my hypothesis, what would I expect to occur?" Indirect confirmation asks, "If I acted in conflict with my hypothesis, what would I expect to occur?" If Taylor had stopped with the first question, we'd all be fiddling with the lights. Only the second question allowed him to discover the deeper truth.

Contrast Effect

The contrast effect changes one's normal perception as a result of exposure to a stimulus in the same dimension. A number of optical illusions work by exploiting the contrast effect.

In the image above, the two inner rectangles are the same shade of gray, but the top one looks lighter because of the contrast with the background.

In interpersonal relationships, the contrast effect means that we judge the current state of the relationship by its contrast to an earlier state. If someone has been enormously attentive and is now less so (even if much more so than the average person), this change is perceived disproportionately negatively. If someone has been cold or distant and warms up even slightly (but less so than the first person), that's perceived disproportionately positively.

Cryptomnesia

Robert Louis Stevenson refers to an incident of cryptomnesia that took place during the writing of *Treasure Island*, and that he discovered to his embarrassment several years afterward:

> *I am now upon a painful chapter. No doubt the parrot once belonged to Robinson Crusoe. No doubt the skeleton is conveyed from Poe. I think little of these, they are trifles and details; and no man can hope to have a monopoly of skeletons or make a corner in talking birds. The stockade, I am told, is from Masterman Ready. It may be, I care not a jot. These useful writers had fulfilled the poet's saying: departing, they had left behind them Footprints on the sands of time, Footprints which perhaps another—and I was the other! It is my debt to Washington Irving that exercises my conscience, and justly so, for I believe plagiarism was rarely carried farther. I chanced to pick up the Tales of a Traveller some years ago with a view to an anthology of prose narrative, and the book flew up and struck me: Billy Bones, his chest, the company in the parlour, the whole inner spirit, and a good deal of the material detail of my first chapters—all were there, all were the property of Washington Irving. But I had no guess of it then as I sat writing by the fireside, in what seemed the spring-tides of a somewhat pedestrian inspiration; nor yet day by day, after lunch, as I read aloud my morning's work to the family. It seemed to me original as sin; it seemed to belong to me like my right eye.*

Sometimes what seems like inspiration turns out to be memory, and you've committed inadvertent plagiarism, or cryptoamnesia. In a 1989 study, people generated examples (such as kinds of birds), and later were asked to create new examples and to recall which answers they had previously personally given. Between 3 to 9 percent of the time, people either listed examples previously given or recalled as their own someone else's thought.

Few writers would risk committing deliberate plagiarism, but the dangers of cryptoamnesia are real. It's most likely to occur when you don't have the ability to monitor your sources properly, when you're away from the original source of the idea, or when the idea was originally suggested by a person of the same sex! It's also likely to happen in a brainstorming session, in which you recall as yours an idea that came up immediately before your idea.

Of course, not all claims of cryptoamnesia are necessarily valid; sometimes the plagiarism was all too deliberate. But nothing else explains certain situations in which people with an awful lot to lose commit what appears to be blatant plagiarism with no upside whatsoever.

The courts have ruled that the unconsciousness of the plagiarism doesn't excuse it. The classic (rock) case is *Bright Tunes Music v. Harri-songs Music,* a 1976 lawsuit involving the similarities between the 1963 song "He's So Fine" and Harrison's own 1969 "My Sweet Lord."

That judgment from that suit cost George Harrison $587,000.

Cognitive biases can be expensive.

D

Déformation Professionnelle
Your training as a professional carries with it an intrinsic bias that's often expressed by the phrase "when the only tool you have is a hammer, all problems look like nails." We probably know IT professionals who think every problem can be best solved with software, human resources professionals who think every problem yields to training and human capital development, and project managers who think all problems lie inside the confines of the triple constraints. Each profession, of course, provides enormous value, but no single profession has all the answers.

Denomination Effect
One way to limit your daily spending is to carry only large denomination bills. Research shows that people are less likely to spend larger bills than their equivalent value in smaller ones.

Disposition Effect

Markets are supposed to be rational, but investors aren't, according to the discipline of behavior finance. Investors have a tendency to sell shares whose price has increased but hold onto assets that have dropped in value, because the pain of recognizing losses exceeds the potential pleasure of having assets that may yet grow. The disposition effect is measure of that tendency.

Distinction Bias

In sales, it's well known that if you present the customer with the higher-priced option first, the customer will be happier with his or her final decision, regardless of which choice he or she finally makes.

The distinction bias is the observed difference between how people evaluate options side by side and how people evaluate the same options when presented separately. If you look at two 52-inch high-definition television sets side by side, any quality difference between them looms large indeed, and paying the money for the "better" one seems sensible.

But if you evaluate the sets separately, you may not notice any material quality difference at all. If so, and if both sets are good enough, you're more likely to buy the cheaper one. So before buying a big ticket item, make sure you evaluate your options separately. You may make a very different decision.

E

Egocentric Bias

There are two different types of egocentric bias: social and memory.

The social egocentric bias makes people tend to take more credit for their own part of a joint action than an outside observer would give them. What's interesting about the egocentric bias is that people not only claim more credit for positive outcomes (which would make this the same as "self-serving bias") but also claim more responsibility for negative outcomes.

The memory egocentric bias is a self-serving tendency to remember our own past in a way that makes us look better. Like most memory biases, this isn't the same thing as lying about our past; it's a form of self-deception in which we really do recall things that way, facts notwithstanding.

Endowment Effect
The endowment effect is also found in behavioral economics, where it's also called "divestiture aversion." In one test, people demanded a much higher price to sell a coffee mug they'd been given than they were willing to pay for a coffee mug they didn't yet own. This contradicts a standard principle of economic theory that a person's willingness to pay (WTP) should be equal to his or her willingness to accept payment (WTA).

There are arguments about why this is so. One possibility is that emotional attachments to things you already own may make them seem more valuable to you. It's also been linked to a form of "status quo bias," a general dislike of change. Some other experiments have not detected this effect.

Experimenter's Bias
This bias is well known to anyone in scientific fields. It's the tendency for experimenters to believe and trust data that agrees with their hypothesis and to disbelieve and distrust data that doesn't. It's a natural enough feeling; there's a price to pay if we're wrong, even if it's only a hit to our egos. It's impossible for any human being to be completely objective. Our perceptions and intelligence are constrained, and we are looking from the inside, not the outside.

Experimenter's bias can't be avoided; instead, it has to be managed. To do so, you have to recognize that you have biases. Self-awareness helps. Another good technique is the "buddy system." Michael frequently works with coauthors, so he has someone to challenge my thinking. That reduces the problem, though it doesn't eliminate it—wherever the coauthors share the same bias, the risk remains.

Extraordinarity Bias
A cheese sandwich that appears to have the image of the Virgin Mary on it isn't tastier than one without, but a normal cheese sandwich costs a couple of bucks while the one with the Virgin sold for $28,000. A guitar once owned by Elvis Presley might not play better (or possibly even as well) as a new one, but people are willing to pay much more for it.

That's not wrong, it's simply a bias. The extraordinarity bias is the measure of your willingness to pay more (sometimes much more) for an "extraordinarity" of an object that doesn't in itself change the intrinsic value of the object. The extraordinarity can be personal as well as external. A present from a loved one, for example, could have far more value to you than the intrinsic object is worth.

There's no reason to avoid the extraordinarity bias. The only thing you need to do is to be conscious of it.

F–Z

For More, Join Our Conversation

This only takes us through the letter *e*. For the nearly 100 additional cognitive biases, join us on our blog at sidewiseinsights.blogspot.com.

Bibliography

Ambrose, Stephen, *Eisenhower: Soldier and President* (condensed version), New York: Simon & Schuster, 1990.

——, *Nothing Like It in the World: The Men Who Built the Transcontinental Railroad 1863–1869*, New York: Simon & Schuster, 2001.

Barrow, John D., *Impossibility: The Limits of Science and the Science of Limits*, New York: Oxford University Press, 1999.

Black, Conrad, *Franklin Delano Roosevelt: Champion of Freedom*, New York: Public Affairs, 2003.

Block, Peter, *The Answer to How Is Yes: Acting on What Matters*, San Francisco: Berrett-Koehler Publishers, 2003.

Caro, Robert A., *The Power Broker: Robert Moses and the Fall of New York*, New York: Alfred A. Knopf, 1974.

Clarke, Arthur C., *Greetings, Carbon-Based Bipeds! Collected Essays 1934–1998*, New York: St. Martin's Press, 1999.

Crawford, Matthew B., *Shop Class as Soulcraft: An Inquiry into the Value of Work*, New York: Penguin, 2009.

Dobson, Michael, and Deborah Singer Dobson, *Enlightened Office Politics: Understanding, Coping With, and Winning the Game—Without Losing Your Soul,* New York: AMACOM, 2001.

Dobson, Michael, and Heidi Feickert, *The Six Dimensions of Project Management: Turning Constraints into Resources,* Vienna, VA: Management Concepts, 2007.

Earnest, Peter, and Maryann Karinch, *Business Confidential: Powerful Lessons for Corporate Success from Inside the CIA,* New York: AMACOM, 2010.

Fisher, Roger, and William Ury, *Getting to Yes: Negotiating Agreement Without Giving In* (second edition), New York: Penguin, 1991.

Hartley, Robert F., *Marketing Mistakes,* 3rd Ed., New York: John Wiley & Sons, 1986.

Johansson, Frans, *The Medici Effect: What Elephants and Epidemics Can Teach Us About Innovation,* Boston: Harvard Business Press, 2006.

Kidder, Rushworth M., *How Good People Make Tough Choices: Resolving the Dilemmas of Ethical Living,* New York: HarperCollins (Quill), 1995.

McCullough, David, *The Great Bridge: The Epic Story of the Building of the Brooklyn Bridge,* New York: Simon & Schuster, 2001.

Mirza, Humayun, *From Plassey to Pakistan,* 2nd Ed., Washington, D.C.: University Press of America, 2002.

Naisbitt, John, *Mind Set! Eleven Ways to Change the Way You See —and Create —the Future,* New York: Harper Paperbacks, 2008.

Niles, Douglas, and Michael Dobson, *Fox on the Rhine,* New York: Forge, 2000.

Nuland, Sherwin B., *The Doctor's Plague: Germs, Childbed Fever, and the Strange Story of Ignac Semmelweis (Great Discoveries),* New York: W. W. Norton: 2003.

Project Management Institute, *A Guide to the Project Management Body of Knowledge (PMBOK Guide),* 3rd Ed., Newtown Square, PA: Project Management Institute, 2004.

Roth, Daniel, "Driven: Shai Agassi's Audacious Plan to Put Electric Cars on the Road," *Wired* magazine 16:09, August 2008.

Sobel, Robert, *When Giants Stumble: Classic Business Blunders and How to Avoid Them,* Paramus, NJ: Prentice Hall, 1999.

Woodward, Bob, *State of Denial: Bush at War, Part III,* New York: Simon & Schuster, 2006.

Index

About the Authors

 **Michael Dobson** is the author of 21 books ranging from project management to World War II military thrillers. A former game company executive, Dobson has led creative project teams in new product development, marketing, and publicity. He was part of the research team that built the Smithsonian National Air and Space Museum, co-won the H. G. Wells Award for simulation design, and currently lectures and teaches internationally on project management and business creativity.

 **Ted Leemann** is a leading speaker on project management, having appeared on Forbes SkyRadio and before audiences ranging from the American Society for Training and Development to the International Society for Performance Improvement. Leemann was president of the Center for Systems Management, and during a 23-year Army career he served as director of quality assurance for the Defense Logistic Agency; was an Inspector General for U.S. Army Europe, auditing performance of U.S. forces throughout NATO; and was a member of the West Point faculty and staff.

About Sidewise Thinking

The world is filled with risk—opportunity and threat—and most of it is only obvious if you know where to look.

Sidewise thinking is the art of learning how to look at the same thing as everyone else and see something different. That's what creative project management is all about.

We started the Sidewise Institute to develop and teach the principles of practical lateral thinking: how to be creative on time, on budget, and to spec. We've developed a network of other sidewise thinkers: a world-class parachute jumper and authority on risk-taking, a former presidential speechwriter on advanced strategic communications, a former military interrogator and expert on how to read people like a book, and more.

For information on keynoting, training, consulting, or other services, visit us at www.sidewiseinsights.com.

Made in the USA
Las Vegas, NV
16 November 2021